THE NEW
MALAYSIAN
HOUSE

ROBERT POWELL

photographs by ALBERT LIM KS

PERIPLUS EDITIONS
Singapore • Hong Kong • Indonesia

Published by Periplus Editions (HK) Ltd, with editorial offices at 61 Tai Seng Avenue #02-12 Singapore 534167.

Text © 2008 Robert Powell
Photographs © 2008 Albert Lim Koon Seng

ISBN: 978-0-7946-0499-8

Author's Note
The convention in Malaysia is to use the terms ground floor, first floor, second floor, etc. rather than first storey, second storey, etc., and this has been adopted throughout the book. All measurements are in metric.

Photographic Credits
All photographs are by Albert Lim KS except for the following: Frank Ling, page 105 top; Satoshi Asakawa (reproduced here with permission of Frank Ling of Architron Design Consultants), pages 78 top, 81 top, 100–1, 102, 106–7, 108 top, 109 and 110 top.

Distributed by:
North America, Latin America and Europe
Tuttle Publishing
364 Innovation Drive
North Clarendon, VT 05759-9436 U.S.A.
Tel: 1 (802) 773-8930; Fax: 1 (802) 773-6993
info@tuttlepublishing.com
www.tuttlepublishing.com

Japan
Tuttle Publishing
Yaekari Building, 3rd Floor;
5-4-12 Osaki; Shinagawa-ku; Tokyo 141 0032
Tel: (81) 03 5437-0171; Fax: (81) 03 5437-0755
tuttle-sales@gol.com

Asia Pacific
Berkeley Books Pte Ltd,
61 Tai Seng Avenue #02-12, Singapore 534167
Tel: (65) 6280-1330; Fax: (65) 6280-6290
inquiries@periplus.com.sg
www.periplus.com

Printed in Hong Kong
10 09 08   6 5 4 3 2

Front endpaper A channel of water springs from a small fountain and tumbles over a weir alongside the patio— Tierra House (page 100).

Back endpaper The exquisite ceiling in the master bedroom of the Wooi House (page 48).

Page 1 A towering column is at the heart of the Wooi House (page 48).

Page 2 The Setiamurni House (page 30) is a meticulously detailed dwelling, tailored to the requirements of an investment banker.

Pages 4–5 The X2 House (page 136) exploits a steep slope.

Pages 6–7 Lydia's House (page 82); Lee House (page 188); Safari Roof House (page 66).

Contents

the new malaysian house

'THE HISTORY OF ARCHITECTURE CAN BE UNDERSTOOD THROUGH INDIVIDUAL HOUSES. IN THEM THERE IS ALWAYS SOMETHING EXPERIMENTAL, HEDONISTIC … PROVOCATIVE.' *Elias Torres Turi*[1]

Collectively, the houses in this book demonstrate a remarkable flowering of design genius in Malaysia at the beginning of the twenty-first century. The dwellings range from detached residences set in extensive landscaped gardens to extended family compounds, and from houses in the gated communities that are springing up in Kuala Lumpur and elsewhere in Malaysia to weekend retreats in the rainforest. All the houses are distinguished by the singular quality of exemplary design.

In the 1980s, architectural debate in Asia revolved around the notions of 'identity'[2] and 'critical regionalism'.[3] The subsequent discourse about the 'global' and the 'local' fuelled several publications in the 1990s, such as *The Asian House*,[4] *The Tropical Asian House*[5] and *Contemporary Vernacular*,[6] which placed the production of architect-designed dwellings within a broad theoretical framework.

Malaysian participants in the various seminars that were convened at that time included Ken Yeang and Jimmy CS Lim. Their approaches to domestic architecture were at different ends of a spectrum of regionalism. Yeang's influential white concrete-framed Roof-Roof House in Selangor (1984) employed a totally modern language while Jimmy CS Lim's romantic Precima House in Bangsar (1988) illustrated a neo-vernacular approach. The earlier Tengku Adlin House in Kota Kinabalu (1978) by Lee Seng Loong was also notable for its lucid interpretation of modern architecture, modified by climate and cultural response. By the end of the twentieth century, the Dialogue House at Bangi Golf Resort (1997) by Frank Ling and Pilar Gonzalez-Herraiz of Architron Design

Consultants[7] was described by its designers as an exploration of 'the ritual responses and events emanating from relationships', while Pat's House at Sierramas (1995–9) by Lim Teng Ngiom investigated a 'climate sensitive modernism' and the notion of 'inflections'.[8] Meanwhile, Chan Soo Khian produced the memorable Heeren House in Malacca (1999), which powerfully evoked memories as it revealed architecture as a palimpsest.[9] The diversity of these approaches laid the foundations for the explosion of ideas in the first years of the new millennium.

HOUSES IN THE HUMID TROPICS

'HOUSES OF THE WEALTHY BECOME PART OF THE DOMAIN OF SIGNS ON WHICH ALL ARCHITECTS DRAW TODAY. THE PRESENCE OF SUCH EXEMPLARS IS WHAT DEFINES BOTH THE ASPIRATIONS OF PEOPLE AND THE CONSCIOUSNESS OF ARCHITECTS.' *Ismail Serageldin*[10]

For an architect, the design of an individual family dwelling is a demanding yet ultimately rewarding task. Rarely will the designer have such a close relationship with the end user. The most successful houses arise out of a strong empathy between the client and designer. This compatibility is of critical importance because a house is ultimately 'a social portrait of its owner'.

The houses of the wealthy often acquire a hold on the imagination of generations of architects and are transmitted around the world. Think, for example, of the Sarabhai House in Ahmedabad by Le Corbusier (1955) or Gerrit Rietveld's Schroeder House in Utrecht (1923–4). In a similar manner, Jimmy CS Lim's design for the Salinger House at Bangi (1993) was important for its pursuit of an architecture related to Islamic tenets, and like the Eu House in Singapore (1993) by Ernesto Bedmar and Geoffrey Bawa's Cinnamon Hill House at

Lunuganga (1993), it fired the imagination of young architects in Southeast Asia.

In 1996, in *The Tropical Asian House*, I summarized the attributes of a dwelling in the humid tropics. The first three criteria were articulated in a discussion with the late Geoffrey Bawa.[11] Bawa maintained, first of all, that a house in a hot/wet climate (or more specifically a monsoon climate) is about living in close proximity to the natural world. His own designs often revolved around open-to-sky courtyards. Bawa went further and said that a house in the tropics should not destroy any substantial trees on the site. Thirdly, he said, a house in the tropics should be designed with the minimal use of glass.

The other attributes include gardens and non-reflective surfaces to reduce radiated heat, wide overhanging eaves to provide shade, the absence of gutters, in-between spaces in the form of verandahs, terraces and shaded balconies, tall rooms to create thermal air mass and provide thermal insulation, permeable walls facing prevailing winds to give natural ventilation, and plans that are one room deep with openings on opposite sides capable of being adjusted to promote natural ventilation by the 'venturi' effect.

Although these criteria are of profound relevance in Malaysia, the urban house cannot be so pure. I acknowledged that to this list must be added others, namely duality between the public side of a house and the private side. This is tied in with the notion of security, with the public side being 'closed' and the private side 'open'. Pollution, noise and increasingly high temperatures in cities often necessitate air conditioning in some parts of a house.

THE HOUSES IN THIS BOOK

'THE CULTURAL DEFINITION OF THE PRIVATE HOUSE IS UNDERGOING GREAT CHANGE, A TRANSFORMATION THAT, IN ITSELF, CAN GENERATE SIGNIFICANT ARCHITECTURAL INVENTIONS.' *Terence Riley*[12]

The houses in this book illustrate the work of more than twenty practising architects, ranging from doyens of the profession such as Jimmy CS Lim and Ken Yeang to relatively new arrivals on the architectural scene in Malaysia such as Kevin Low's smallprojects, John Ding and Ken Wong's Unit One Design, David Chan Weng Cheong and Chan Mun Inn's DCA (Design Collective Architecture Network) and Wooi Lok Kuang's Wooi Architects.

As varied as the practices are, so too are the design solutions, ranging from the 'unfinished' quality of the Safari Roof House by Kevin Low of smallprojects to the utterly romantic Serendah House by Haris bin Othman of RDA-Harris Architects. The orthogonal precision of the Setiamurni House by Chan Soo Khian of SCDA Architects contrasts with the tilting surfaces and robust materials employed in the X1 House by Lim Teng Ngiom of Ngiom Partnership. Tierra House by Frank Ling and Pilar Gonzalez-Herraiz of Architron Design

Consultants is a fragmented assemblage of forms that subverts conventional notions of dwellings, while landscape architect Ng Seksan is responsible for Sekeping Serendah, a contemporary vernacular weekend house in steel and glass in a rainforest setting.

A number of non-Malaysians working in Southeast Asia have also made contributions to the development of the New Malaysian House, notably Kerry Hill with his design for the strikingly modern Bukit Ledang House, Ernesto Bedmar with the design of the sensuous, layered Sadeesh House and the expansive Lurah Tunku House, and John Bulcock with the elegant and understated Pixie House.

I have structured the book in five sections: Detached Houses, Extended Family Houses, Houses in Gated Settlements, Refurbished Houses and Second Homes and Retreats. This is, admittedly, a post-rationalization of the house types I encountered but each type appears to be driven by different imperatives and to reflect changing cultural practices.

DETACHED HOUSES

'THROUGHOUT HISTORY THE PRIVATE HOUSE HAS PLAYED [A] ROLE. UNLIKE LARGE PROJECTS, WHICH NORMALLY REQUIRE BROADER SOCIETAL, CORPORATE OR POLITICAL CONSENSUS, THE PRIVATE HOUSE CAN BE REALIZED THROUGH THE EFFORTS OF A FEW PEOPLE. IT OFTEN EXPRESSES, IN THE MOST UNCOMPROMISING WAY POSSIBLE, THE VISION OF A CLIENT OR ARCHITECT, OR BOTH.' *Terence Riley*[13]

Included in the first section of the book, devoted to single detached houses, are eight radical new dwellings in and around Kuala Lumpur. The Lurah Tunku House and the Sadeesh House, both designed by Ernesto Bedmar, explore inside/outside relationships and the ambiguous edge that are fundamental to residential design in the tropics. The Setiamurni House by Chan Soo Khian employs the architect's compositional skills in a critical interpretation of contextual modernism, while the Bukit Ledang House by Kerry Hill continues the architect's development of 'a regional modern architecture that accommodates the traditions of the East'. The Wooi House by Wooi Lok Kuang is 'an exploration of materiality, light and space', while the Safari Roof House designed by Kevin Low is, in the architect's words, 'a reconciliation between modernism,

context and culture'. The Caracol House by Frank Ling and Pilar Gonzalez-Herraiz primarily addresses 'the physical and psychological needs of the client'. Finally, the sculptural form of Lydia's House by David Chan Weng Cheong and Chan Mun Inn of DCA is a modernist solution that simultaneously responds to the equatorial climate.

The challenge facing architects in Kuala Lumpur, as in other burgeoning cities in Southeast Asia, is to design houses that permit their clients to live a relaxed lifestyle with open verandahs, terraces and open-to-sky spaces that simultaneously solve issues of security. Living in a conurbation necessitates a variety of responses to the perceived and real threat of intruders, including high perimeter walls and fences, electronic surveillance devices and, in many instances, guards. A house in the city invariably includes some means of isolating and securing the family sleeping quarters at night.

The eight houses are utterly private places. They provide a haven of calm and a 'refuge' from the frantic pace of life in the metropolis. Hasan-Uddin Khan has described such houses as 'fortresses of solitude'.[14] These houses embody a hierarchy of privacy with a public façade that seeks not to attract undue attention or to make an extravagant display of wealth, and interior spaces that embrace and shelter their occupants while opening out to courtyards and terraces.

EXTENDED FAMILY HOUSES

'THE REGIONALLY UNIQUE FAMILY COMPOUND … MERITS FAR GREATER ANALYSIS THAN HAS BEEN GIVEN TO IT AS YET.… ARE THE SPACES AS LAYERED AND VEILED AS THEY APPEAR TO BE? HOW DO THEY ALLOW FOR THE SUBTLE RANGES OF "KNOWING" AND "CHOOSING-NOT-TO-KNOW" THAT MUST CHARACTERISE THE RELATIONSHIPS BETWEEN THE THREE GENERATIONS OF THE FAMILY THAT INHABIT A COMMUNE?' *Leon van Schaik*[15]

Societies in Southeast Asia place great value on filial piety and it is not uncommon to encounter three generations of a family living together. Elsewhere I have described Bann Ton Son, a three-generation family compound in Bangkok designed by Prapapat and Theeraphon Niyom (1990), and another three-generation complex for the Hadiprana family at Tanah Gajah to the east of Ubud in Bali (1989).[16] The Sennett House in Singapore (2000) designed by Chan Soo Khian was also built for a married brother and sister and their families who share a compound with their mother.[17] Likewise, the U3 House in Bangkok (1997) designed by Kanika Ratanapridakul is the home of the architect, her sister and their parents.[18]

The multigenerational home presents a number of challenges for the designer. There are hierarchies of privacy to consider and it is necessary to understand the relationships between members of the family. A balance has to be maintained between intimate and private space and shared space that reflects the family structure.

The tradition of grandparents living with their children and grandchildren is also an enduring phenomenon in Malaysia and three of the houses in the book demonstrate solutions to this mutually supportive form of living. David Chan Weng Chong and Chan Mun Inn have designed the Ambi House at Nilai for an extended family of artists and writers who collaborate in their creative work. The Tierra House by Frank Ling and Pilar Gonzalez-Herraiz is tailor-made for a 'large extended family with regular visiting relatives' at Saujana Resort in Shah Alam. And the Johor House designed by John Ding and Ken Wong is a compound embracing five separate dwellings housing four siblings and their parents on a site close to the 'second causeway' to Singapore.

HOUSES IN GATED SETTLEMENTS

'A HOUSE SERVES MAN IN TWO BASIC WAYS; IT OFFERS HIM REFUGE WHERE HE CAN FEEL AT HOME AND BE AT PEACE WITH HIMSELF, AND IT SERVES AS A STARTING POINT FOR HIS ACTIONS IN THE WORLD … WHEN THE HOUSE CREATES A SENSE OF BELONGING AND PROTECTION MAN GAINS THE INNER STRENGTH HE NEEDS TO DEPART.' *Christian Norberg-Shultz*[19]

The twenty-first century has witnessed the proliferation of gated settlements. In part, this is a response to rising crime rates that have accompanied surging economic growth in Southeast Asian cities. Protection of family, in particular children, is high on every house owner's priorities. Gated settlements are one response to this situation, in effect recreating what has been metaphorically likened to

the 'medieval fortress' with 'walls' in the form of boundary fences, and security guards at the entrance gate accompanied by centralized CCTV surveillance, with cameras fixed at strategic locations.[20] Entry is restricted to the residents, their invited guests and employees.

The six houses illustrated in the third section of the book are all located in gated communities in the greater Kuala Lumpur conurbation. Three of the houses – the X1 House, the X2 House and the Wong Soo House – are built within the protected confines of Sierramas at Sungai Buloh. The Fathil House overlooks the fairways at The Mines Resort. Similarly, the Pixie House is located at Lakeview Bungalows, a development adjacent to the internationally renowned Saujana Golf Resort. The Louvrebox House is to be found at Gita Bayu.

The creation of a secure environment within a gated settlement is intended to encourage the removal of front boundary walls and the acceptance of so-called 'green streets' within the settlements, thereby facilitating community interaction. The result is a more open frontage although 'walls' creep back in covert ways and most houses turn inwards to private internal spaces.

In a sense, those who elect to live within a protected compound are 'victims' of Malaysia's economic success and the divisions that this has exacerbated in society. The perimeter wire fences not only keep intruders at arm's length but, ironically, 'imprison' the residents in a controlled environment that restricts their 'freedom' to participate in the city.

REFURBISHED HOUSES

'A HOUSE IS NEVER "FINISHED", IT MUST ALLOW FOR GROWTH AND CHANGE FOR A HOUSE IS AN ORGANIC THING…. IT MUTATES AND CHANGES AND GROWS OLD…. MY PREFERENCES CHANGE EVERY YEAR … AND IF MY HOUSE IS UNFINISHED [IT] WILL CATER FOR THE CHANGE.' *Ng Seksan*[21]

Many house owners choose to refurbish an existing house rather than relocate or build anew, especially if it is in a desirable or accessible location. The refurbishment frequently involves the radical reconfiguration of an existing structure in response to an evolving lifestyle, changes in family structure or simply the need for more accommodation. The

desire to renovate may equally stem from an attachment to a dwelling that has memorable associations with family and significant events. The best house plans have a robustness that permits change.

Buildings are a resource embodying energy so that refurbishment and extension can also be seen as a sustainable practice. I have written elsewhere about the house of Jimmy CS Lim in Kuala Lumpur.[22] It has been in a constant state of growth for thirty years and has valuable lessons to teach about resource conservation, recycling, continuity and evolution.

Three houses are featured in the section on refurbished dwellings. They are all 1960s residences that have been radically transformed and in their reincarnation have adjusted to contemporary requirements.

The Bilis House by John Ding and Ken Wong is a generic solution, injecting new vigour into a ubiquitous terrace house, while the reconfiguration of the Lee House by architect Chris Lee for his mother evokes memories of a family life that revolved around the swimming pool. In contrast, the internal rearrangement and extension of the Jalan Tempinis Satu House by Ng Seksan is a response to the needs of the owner's changed circumstances. It has been transformed from a bachelor's residence into a bustling family home. In the process, the house has become a palimpsest, embodying layers of family history and memories.

SECOND HOMES AND RETREATS

'PERHAPS … IT WILL BECOME MORE COMMON FOR PEOPLE TO SPEND LESS ON THEIR HOMES-WORKPLACES AND SAVE THEIR EARNINGS TO BUY WEEKEND HOUSES, THEREBY REINTEGRATING SOLITUDE INTO AN OTHERWISE WIRED WORLD?'
Terence Riley[23]

The rapid growth of Asian cities and the accompanying problems of increased density, traffic congestion and pollution have seen the proliferation of a parallel phenomenon – second homes. When city dwellers have sufficient means to escape the frenetic pace of life in the city they acquire a site, some distance from the city, to build a second home. Preferably the site will be off the beaten track, yet accessible, and though somewhat isolated, not without basic services.

Two of the houses in the last section of the book lie some 35 kilometres northeast of Kuala Lumpur at Janda Baik, off the Karak Highway on the way to Kuantan. The Enderong House by Ngan Ching Woo and the Sum Sum Valley House by Choo Gim Wah are both located in the Tanarimba development at Janda Baik that has been masterminded by architect Ngan Ching Woo.

The other three houses are located at Serendah, 40 kilometres north of the capital and accessed by the Kuala

Lumpur–Ipoh Highway. The Serendah House is a weekend retreat designed by Abdul Haris bin Othman, while Sekeping Serendah is a modern translation of a jungle hut located in the rainforest. Close by are two Mud Houses designed by Kevin Low that experiment with laterite clay as a building material.

All five houses, located approximately 45 minutes' drive from Kuala Lumpur, offer the opportunity to escape the stress of city life, to relax, to enjoy the natural environment, to revitalise the body and to restore the soul. In the evening, a deep silence descends in the forest and all five houses are utterly secluded.

THE RETURN OF THE NATIVE

'ONE OF THE PRINCIPAL ISSUES OF DESIGNING IN THE TROPICS IS THE DISCOVERY OF A DESIGN LANGUAGE OF LINE, EDGE, MESH AND SHADE RATHER THAN AN ARCHITECTURE OF PLANE, SOLID AND VOID. AN (UN)-LEARNING PROCESS IS INVOLVED, GIVEN THE DOMINANCE OF EUROPEAN ARCHITECTURE WHICH FORMS THE SUBSTANCE OF THE TRAINING OF ARCHITECTS OVER THE PAST 200 YEARS.' *Tay Kheng Soon*[24]

It is significant that every architect whose work is featured in this book has received part of his or her education overseas and has worked for a period outside Malaysia. Six of the sixteen Malaysian-born architects attended architectural schools in Australia, six in the UK and four in the US. After some years they have returned to their country of birth to be confronted with what Tay Kheng Soon has described as 'a process of (un)learning', where a new language must be assimilated in which 'the building section takes precedence over the plan as the generator of building form and the basis of design thinking'.[25]

Some of the 'new generation' of Malaysian architects pursued their architectural education in the Antipodes, at Curtin University of Technology, Sydney University, the University of New South Wales, RMIT University, the University of Adelaide and Lincoln University at Canterbury in New Zealand. Others took a route that led them to the USA and Yale University, MIT, the University of Oregon, Miami University in Ohio and Washington University. A third group chose to further their architectural studies in the UK at the

Architectural Association, Cambridge University, the University of North London, the University of Wales and the University of London.

The early masters of the modern movement have evidently been a significant influence on many of this generation of architects. Le Corbusier, Marcel Breuer, Hans Scharoun, Rudolf Schindler, Mies van der Rohe, Alvar Aalto and Louis Kahn are frequently referred to, as are Frank Lloyd Wright and Carlo Scarpa. Architects who have trained in Australia frequently recall the more recent works of Kerry Hill, Peter Stutchbury and Richard Leplastrier.

Academic mentors have also been an important source of inspiration, so that theoretical constructs and design methodologies can often be traced back to influential professors such as Ian McHarg at the University of Pennsylvania, Ronald Lewcock at MIT, Patrick O'Sullivan at the University of Wales, Alan Balfour and Peter Cook at the AA, Florien Beigal at the London Metropolitan University and Nevile D'Cruz at Curtin University of Technology.

Inspiration has also come from outside the architectural discipline. Kevin Low acknowledges the influence on his work of the artist Andy Goldsworthy, while Frank Ling and Pilar Gonzalez-Herraiz refer to the thought-provoking films of Fellini, Altman and Tarkovsky. Landscape architects such as Martha Schwartz and Per Gustavson have provided stimulus and engineers Frei Otto and Ove Arup are singled out for praise.

Equally, the authority of Asian 'Masters' such as Geoffrey Bawa, Balkrishna V. Doshi and Tadao Ando is acknowledged, and pioneering Malaysian architects such as Kamil Merican, Jimmy CS Lim and Ken Yeang have inspired and, in some instances, mentored the present generation.

EVOLVING IDEAS

'[THERE IS] … A GROWING CONSENSUS THAT THE NEW ARCHITECTURE IF IT IS TO MEET THE CHALLENGE OF THE ENVIRONMENTAL CRISIS, ASIDE FROM MORE PAROCHIAL ISSUES, MUST BE FIRMLY GROUNDED IN ECOLOGICAL PRINCIPLES. AT THE VERY LEAST IT SHOULD BE TROPICAL ARCHITECTURE, RESPONSIVE TO AND EXPRESSIVE OF ITS GEOGRAPHICAL AND CLIMATIC SITUATION. THE TECHNOLOGICAL MEANS

Right The modest entrance of the X1 House (page 126) conceals a surprisingly large dwelling.

FOR ACHIEVING THIS END RANGE FROM THE EMPLOY-
MENT OF TIMBER-FRAMED STRUCTURES UPDATED
FROM TRADITIONAL MODELS, TO HIGH-TECH MATERI-
ALS AND TECHNIQUES OF PRODUCTION.' *Chris Abel*[26]

In a world where climate change and carbon emissions will impact upon every region and every country, there is evidence of an increasing awareness of the responsibility of architects to build in a sustainable manner. The houses in this book show a firm grasp of the principles of designing with climate. They are concerned with orientation in relation to the sun path and to wind. Overhanging eaves are part of the vocabulary that most architects draw upon, as are high ceilings, louvred walls and the use of the 'skin' of the building as a permeable filter.

It is evident too that architects appreciate that buildings in the tropics should be designed in section rather than in plan. The roof is frequently the most important element in the design of a house, providing shade from the sun and shelter from the monsoon rains. Water is incorporated into a number of dwellings and increasingly it is recycled. In a number of houses, a wind shaft creating a 'stack' effect enhances ventilation.

Forested hills form a backdrop to almost every house in this book. Many of the houses are built on hillsides and exploit the topography to create imaginative sections. Landscape is an integral part of every house, whether in the dense urban setting or a secluded weekend retreat away from the city.

Some things never change, in so far as the sun path and the wind direction in the geographical context of Malaysia are always givens. What is changing is the flow of ideas about how to live in the twenty-first century – such as changing cultural patterns and greater awareness of environmental issues – and this is resulting in new and often unconventional dwellings in the Malaysian context.

What we are witnessing is the emergence of design talent that has been germinating since the mid-1980s. In the 1990s it was sporadic in its manifestations. Now it has materialized in an abundance of confident and exhilarating expressions.

[1] Elias Torres Tur, 'Thoughts about Architecture', in Phillipa Baker (ed.), *Architecture and Polyphony: Building in the Islamic World Today*, London: Thames & Hudson, 2004, p. 147.

[2] Robert Powell (ed.), *Architecture and Identity: Exploring Architecture in Islamic Cultures*, Vol. 1, The Aga Khan Award for Architecture and Universiti Teknologi Malaysia, Singapore: Concept Media, 1983.

[3] Robert Powell, *Regionalism in Architecture: Exploring Architecture in Islamic Cultures*, Vol. 2, The Aga Khan Award for Architecture and Bangladesh University of Engineering and Technology, Dhaka, Singapore: Concept Media, 1985.

[4] Robert Powell, *The Asian House: Contemporary Houses of Southeast Asia*, Singapore: Select Books, 1993.

[5] Robert Powell, *The Tropical Asian House*, Singapore: Select Books, 1996.

[6] William Siew Wai Lim and Tan Hock Beng, *Contemporary Vernacular*, Singapore: Select Books, 1998.

[7] Robert Powell, *The Urban Asian House: Contemporary Houses of Southeast Asia*, Singapore: Select Books, 1998, pp. 86–95.

[8] Robert Powell, *The New Asian House*, Singapore: Select Books, 2001, pp. 64–9.

[9] Robert Powell, 'Architecture as a Palimpsest', *d+a*, Issue 10, Singapore: SNP Media Asia, 2002.

[10] Ismail Serageldin, 'The Architecture of the Individual House: Understanding the Models', in Robert Powell (ed.), *The Architecture of Housing: Exploring Architecture in Islamic Cultures*, Geneva: The Aga Khan Trust for Culture, 1990, p. 206.

[11] Geoffrey Bawa in conversation with the author, November 1994.

[12] Terence Riley, *The Un-Private House*, New York: Museum of Modern Art, 1999, p. 36.

[13] Ibid., p 28.

[14] Hasan-Uddin Khan, 'The Architecture of the Individual House', in Robert Powell (ed.), *The Architecture of Housing: Exploring Architecture in Islamic Cultures*, Geneva: The Aga Khan Trust for Culture, 1990, p. 175.

[15] Leon van Schaik, *SCDA Architects: A Review*, SIA-GETZ Architecture Prize for Emerging Architecture, Singapore, 2006.

[16] Powell, *The Asian House*, pp. 110–23.

[17] Robert Powell, *The New Singapore House*, Select Books, Singapore, 2001, pp. 114–19.

[18] Robert Powell, *The New Thai House*, Select Books, Singapore, 2003, pp. 90–5.

[19] Christian Norberg-Shultz, *Roots of Modern Architecture*, Tokyo: ADA Edita, 1998, p. 71.

[20] Umberto Eco writes of the 'medievalization of the city' in *Travels in Hyperreality*, London: Picador, 1986, pp. 76–7.

[21] Ng Seksan in conversation with the author, July 2006.

[22] Powell, *The Urban Asian House*, pp. 148–55.

[23] Riley, *The Un-Private House*, p. 35.

[24] Tay Kheng Soon, 'The Architectural Aesthetics of Tropicality', in Robert Powell (ed.), *Modern Tropical Architecture: Line, Edge and Shade*, Singapore: Page One, 1997, p. 13.

[25] Ibid., p. 42.

[26] Chris Abel, *Architecture and Identity*, Oxford: Architectural Press, 1997, p. 195.

lurah tunku house

BUKIT TUNKU, KUALA LUMPUR
ARCHITECT: ERNESTO BEDMAR
BEDMAR AND SHI

The Lurah Tunku House, designed by Argentine-born architect Ernesto Bedmar for a prominent Malaysian businessman, is entered at the eastern end of a 50-metre-long axis that runs along the flank of a hill.

Security at the entrance gatehouse is strictly enforced before visitors are allowed to enter the drive. A vigilant guard sits before an array of video screens that relay pictures from CCTV cameras located around the perimeter fence and at strategic locations within the house. Once inside the compound, however, the security measures become less intrusive and the spatial and tactile qualities of the house assume greater significance.

Passing through the entrance lobby, a broad timber bridge spans a lily pond that is the prelude to the linear route that terminates in an outdoor living room with a verandah overlooking a three-lane-wide Olympic-length swimming pool – an indelible ultramarine 'slash' across the landscape. The pool is perpendicular to the east–west axis and thrusts northwards, flanked by rainforest trees.

Four pavilions are attached to the main axis. The first contains the car porch and a spacious entrance lobby with two guest suites at subbasement level. The second pavilion houses a child's bedroom, a playroom and a study above two more guest rooms. A bridge links the child's suite to the third pavilion that contains an open-to-sky reception area, the master bedroom suite, a study-cum-office and an external north-facing shaded terrace attached to the master bedroom. This latter pavilion is perpendicular to and spans the primary axis.

The fourth pavilion terminates the linear axis with two glass boxes containing the formal dining room and the living room, flanking an open-sided external living area. The rooms look east across a deep, wooded valley. Beneath the living room and dining room, in a subbasement, are the gymnasium, playroom and sauna, with direct access to the pool deck.

Between the third and fourth pavilions, the terrain descends steeply to the north and Bedmar has introduced three broad flights of stairs to create a large 'amphitheatre'. The backcloth to this space is a view to the north of dense forest reserve, although the house is close to

Pages 18–19 Detail of the striated façade of the Setiamurni House (page 30).

Pages 20–1 Space is orchestrated on a grand scale, exploiting the topography to create vistas.

Below The architectural language is distinctly modern, with a restrained palette of materials, including white painted plaster, grey powder-coated aluminium windows, steel, glass and timber.

Right Three broad flights of stairs create a grassy amphitheatre, with the verdant forest as a backcloth.

the centre of Kuala Lumpur. The service areas are screened by a linear palm garden along the southern flank of the principal axis.

Bedmar employs a restrained palette of materials: timber, concrete, steel, white painted plaster and grey powder-coated aluminium window frames. The house exploits the topography to create a multilevel section, and the orchestration of moods is on a grand scale, with extensive vistas out to forested valleys and inwards to palm gardens and rippling ponds. Beneath the haze that frequently envelopes the Malaysian capital, the house appears, at first, somewhat austere but while it lacks the intimacy of some smaller dwellings designed by Bedmar, it is a haven of tranquillity. Working with landforms, the architect explores the inside/ outside relationships that are fundamental to residential design in the tropics.

While most of Ernesto Bedmar's work is located in Singapore, he now has a body of work in Kuala Lumpur and has received commissions in New Delhi, Jakarta, Lhasa (Tibet), London and New York.

Top Wide overhanging eaves protect balconies and windows.

Above On entering the house visitors encounter a broad timber bridge spanning a lily pond. At the end of the bridge is a reception space.

Right An open-sided 50-metre circulation spine links the four pavilions that constitute the plan form.

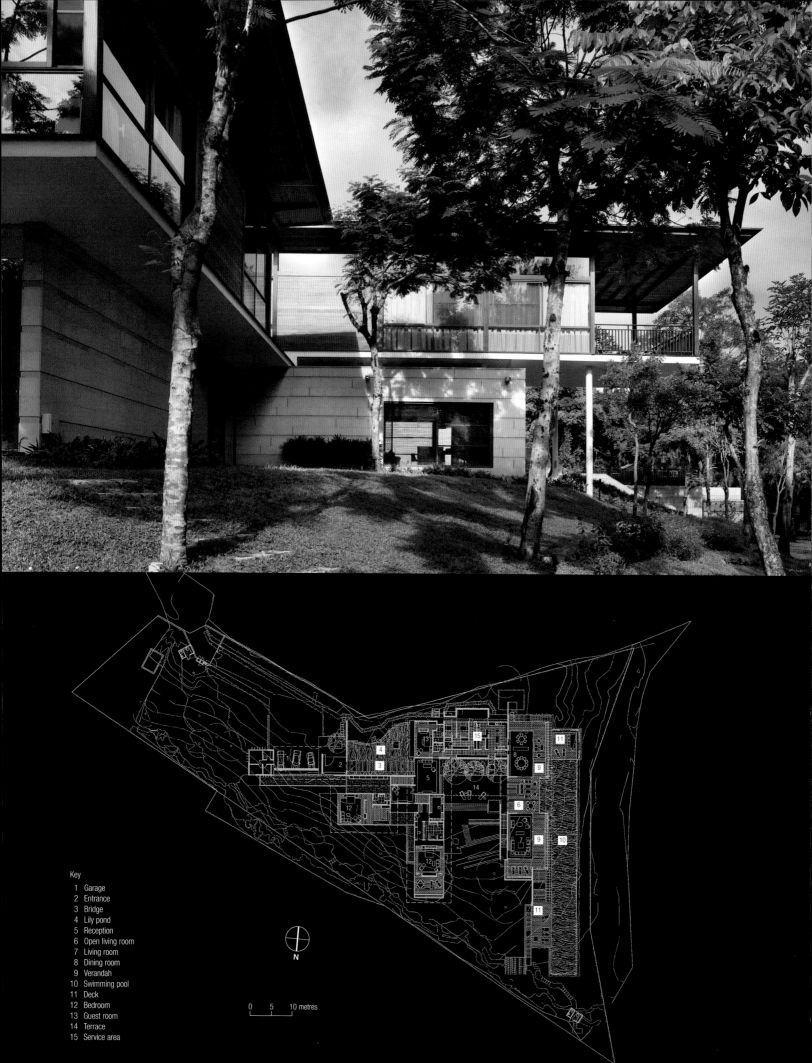

Key
1 Garage
2 Entrance
3 Bridge
4 Lily pond
5 Reception
6 Open living room
7 Living room
8 Dining room
9 Verandah
10 Swimming pool
11 Deck
12 Bedroom
13 Guest room
14 Terrace
15 Service area

N

0   5   10 metres

Left The 'sleeping' pavilion projects out into the landscape.

Below left Ground floor plan.

Right A timber verandah flanks the west façade of the house in close proximity to the forest.

Centre Section through the amphitheatre and circulation spine.

Below The verandah provides opportunities for alfresco dining.

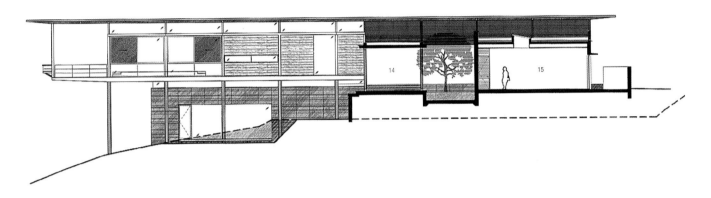

Opposite above Located beneath the master bedroom, the library has direct access to a shaded patio.

Opposite below A three-lane Olympic-length swimming pool slices through the forest, overlooked by a pool deck and gymnasium.

Below The heart of the house is the living room – a haven of tranquillity in close contact with the natural environment.

setiamurni house

BANGSAR, KUALA LUMPUR
ARCHITECT: CHAN SOO KHIAN
SCDA ARCHITECTS

'The design process starts with the careful consideration of programme and site as part of the overall matrix for generation of ideas. The free plan in the design is grounded in classical ideals of scale and proportion. The spaces within the "free plan" overlap and are further defined through the careful placement and clear expression of walls and ceiling planes that intersect with or "slide by" each other. Compositionally these walls propagate from multiple "centres" within the flowing spaces. These "centres" implied within the open concept planning are reinforced when the spaces are experienced sequentially and hierarchically through choreographed processions that recentre and realign the perceptual "axis" that terminates in objects, landscaped vistas or open spaces. These spaces are designed to heighten the experience of sound, touch, smell and sight, unfolding sequentially as one moves through the spaces. Order is emphasized through a clear expression of structure.' CHAN SOO KHIAN

Born and raised in Penang, Chan Soo Khian undertook his architectural education at Washington University and Yale University. Against a backdrop of diverse design philosophies at Yale University's School of Art and Architecture, Chan attempted to ground himself in classicism. The classical language of architecture significantly influenced his development as an architect. It was a focus from which he went on to appreciate the works of the modern masters. Two art galleries at Yale by Louis Kahn were a point of reference for him to develop a structural and spatial vocabulary – a language of volumes and planes enhanced by light and structural order.

Pages 30–1 The open-plan living room enjoys a spectacular view beyond the glass-edged swimming pool to a deep, wooded valley.

Top The open-plan living and dining room has the benefit of excellent natural ventilation when air conditioning is not in use.

Above A separate steel and glass box with timber louvres houses the library and gymnasium.

Right The overhanging roof is supported on composite steel columns. Horizontal aluminium louvres extend along the east and west elevations to counteract the early morning and late evening sun.

Chan worked as an intern with Kohn Pedersen Fox before returning to Asia where he set up a design studio in Singapore in 1995. Two years later he established SCDA Architects. The practice has established a reputation for designing buildings that explore a modern language rooted in the Southeast Asian context.

The Setiamurni House is a rectangular steel and glass pavilion with a distinct horizontal emphasis combining a shallow-pitch flat-seamed aluminium roof above a transparent glass box. Striated grey granite walls, smooth grey oak veneered panels and 300-mm-deep blade-like aluminium louvres reinforce the horizontality. The house is somewhat austere yet strikingly beautiful; it has a personality that is precisely tailored to the requirements of its owner.

Entered in the southeast corner, the site is initially flat and then drops away precipitously along the western boundary. The entrance is from a vehicle court via a bridge that spans a reflective pool and passes over a basement courtyard. The design exploits the views to the west, across a wooded valley, towards the National Science Centre. The huge open-plan living/dining room and a family room are at ground floor level with spectacular views beyond a glass-edged 20-metre-long infinity swimming pool. At first floor level four bedrooms similarly enjoy panoramic views to the west.

The Miesien glass-box aesthetic originated in Europe in the early twentieth century and has undergone considerable transformation to meet the demands of the tropical climate. Here, the wide overhanging roof is supported on strongly articulated composite galvanized steel columns while internally there is a secondary structure of non-directional circular hollow section columns. Horizontal aluminium fins run the length of the east and west elevations to counteract the early morning and the late afternoon sun. The glass walls of the house have full-height aluminium-framed sliding doors that encourage cross-ventilation.

To the north of the main rectangular 'box', the site narrows and this is the location for a detached library and study contained within a smaller steel and glass box with horizontal *chengal* louvres. Accessed by a light steel and glass bridge, the library sits atop a gymnasium within a landscaped garden.

Key
4 Dining room
8 Patio
9 Swimming pool
12 Reflective pool

13 Bedroom
14 Guest room
15 Audio-visual room
16 Verandah

0   5   10 metres

Opposite left The multilayered façade provides sunshading and controlled cross-ventilation.

Opposite right Striated stone cladding reinforces the horizontal emphasis of the elevations.

Top Section through the steeply sloping site.

Above The junctions between materials and their respective functions are expressed with great clarity.

Left The house is simultaneously austere and yet strikingly beautiful.

At subbasement level are two guest rooms with views into a small courtyard and an audio-visual room that opens out to a shaded west-facing verandah. Below the verandah is a concrete retaining wall softened by newly planted palm trees.

Chan is committed to refining a modern architectural language and the Setiamurni House is a sublime interpretation of 'contextual modernism'. It displays the assured manipulation of light, space, structure, transparency and texture that has garnered the architect a number of international awards.

In 2002 Chan received the Architecture Review (UK) Merit Award for Emerging Architecture, an award that confirmed his growing international reputation, a judgement endorsed by the selection of SCDA by Architectural Record (USA) as one of their Year 2003 Design Vanguard firms. And in 2006 he was presented with the SIA–Getz Architecture Prize for Emergent Architecture in Asia.

Left Bedroom suites enjoy views of a wooded valley towards the National Science Centre.

Below left Ensuite bathrooms similarly have magnificent views.

Right The access to the bedrooms on the eastern flank of the house.

Far right The entrance is via a glass-sided bridge over a void that brings light to the guest suites.

Below The precisely detailed kitchen.

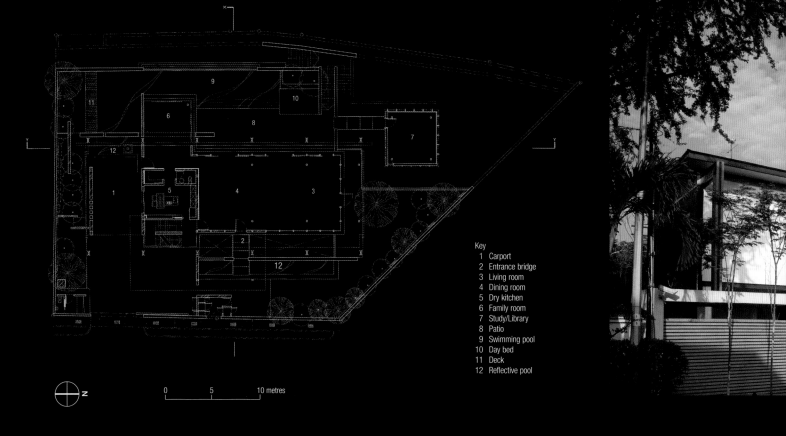

Key

1 Carport
2 Entrance bridge
3 Living room
4 Dining room
5 Dry kitchen
6 Family room
7 Study/Library
8 Patio
9 Swimming pool
10 Day bed
11 Deck
12 Reflective pool

0   5   10 metres

N

Far left Ground floor plan indicating the main living spaces.

Left The house is an exquisitely proportioned steel and glass Miesien pavilion in the tropics.

Right Meticulous detailing in steel, glass, concrete and stone is evident throughout the house.

Below left View of the house from the west. Luxuriant planting softens the high concrete retaining walls that provide security.

Below The swimming pool terrace beyond the living room.

bukit ledang house

FEDERAL HILL, KUALA LUMPUR
ARCHITECT: KERRY HILL
KERRY HILL ARCHITECTS

Located at the foot of Bukit Ledang, in a secluded valley close to the heart of the Malaysian capital, this house is surrounded by steeply rising ground and lofty trees. The access, via a narrow road at the eastern end of the site, passes a security checkpoint before swinging into a paved motor court.

Like other projects by Kerry Hill Architects, the house exhibits a lucid plan. Explaining his desire for clarity, Kerry Hill has said, 'The plan is seen as a mode of distilling elements into a clear diagram, a key to the scheme.'[1] It is an asymmetrical composition of solids, voids and planes relating to a primary axis, with walls extending outwards to frame views of the valley and embrace gardens and paved courts.

A projecting flat-roofed portico gives access to a wide covered gallery, a *promenade architecturale* some 60 metres in length, that runs the length of the house from east to west. This linear route is the principal organizing device, a compositional gambit that Hill has employed in other projects such as the Chedi Lido resort in Java and the Lalu Hotel at Sun Moon Lake in Taiwan.

To the south side of this gallery are three pavilions of varying proportions and height, the first a double-storey reception hall with an adjoining guest suite, the second a formal dining room. Both are linked by flat stone bridges across a linear reflecting pool that runs parallel to the gallery.

A third pavilion, housing the most private family rooms, is set at a slight distance from the other accommodation and terminates the east–west axis. The children's bedrooms at first floor level span over the master bedroom and family room, framing a view of the pool deck beyond. The three pavilions are all one room deep, permitting cross-ventilation, but they also have the option of using air conditioning.

Pages 40–1 The house responds to a site of considerable natural beauty. The forested valley embraces a 25-metre-long swimming pool and a lily pond.

Above An elegant flat-roofed porte-cochere projects into the stone-paved vehicle court.

Above right The second phase of the house includes a spa and a guest suite.

Above far right Simplicity is the keynote of Kerry Hill's reductionist architectural language.

Right A 60-metre-long covered gallery is the principal organizing device of the plan.

To the north of the gallery and concealed behind a timber-clad screen wall are the service spaces: a four-car garage and administrative office, leading to driver and domestic staff accommodation, wet and dry kitchens and food preparation spaces. These spaces can be separately accessed via a walkway running along the north façade of the house.

A singular feature of the house is the spatial separation of functions, although each activity relates to and returns to the dominant east–west axis. The house incorporates a hierarchy of privacy, from the arrival courtyard to the air-conditioned public reception hall, to the dining room and finally to the private and most secure family areas. The principal rooms look into a soft-landscaped courtyard bounded by a low hedge. Eight torches, which can be dramatically ignited in the evening, are arranged in an orthogonal pattern on the lawn outside the dining room.

At the extreme western end is a recreation court with a 25-metre swimming pool. Beyond the low boundary wall that marks the limit of the site, the terrain ascends abruptly, making access almost impossible from the head of the valley.

The second phase of the house, including tennis courts, a guest suite and a small spa, were part of the original design and these have subsequently been added. Conceived as a series of detached pavilions, they are located on the south side of the main axis.

The Bukit Ledang House continues Kerry Hill's development of a regional modern architecture that derives its composition from formal strategies originating in Western modernism overlaying or overlaid by local typologies. The ground floor is predominantly masonry. The first floor is lighter and

is mainly clad in timber with projecting fenestration that simulates traditional monsoon windows, above which overhanging low-pitched hipped roofs are covered with hardwood shingles. Together with the use of louvred timber screens and reflecting pools, they create a richly nuanced materiality that is enhanced by a muted palette of colours.[2] Simplicity is the keynote of the reductionist architectural language but it also engages directly with the tropical climate.

As Geoffrey London has perceptively noted, 'Like an illustrious group of architects from the West – Wright, Le Corbusier, Kahn – Hill's modernist work has been enriched by accommodating the traditions of the East.'[3] The result in the case of the Bukit Ledang House is a dramatic composition that responds magnificently to a site of considerable natural beauty.

Since 1979 Kerry Hill has built a reputable practice based in Singapore and Australia. He has gained the recognition of his peers with a number of awards, including the Aga Khan Award for Architecture (2001) for the design of the Datai Hotel at Pulau Langkawi. In 2006 he was awarded the Gold Medal of the Royal Australian Institute of Architects.

[1] Kerry Hill in a lecture delivered at the University of Western Australia, September 1996.

[2] Robert Powell, 'Nuanced Materiality', The Architectural Review, No. 1265, July 2002, p. 85.

[3] Geoffrey London, 'Earthly Paradise', Monument, No. 41, April/May 2001, p. 80.

Key

1 Entry court
2 Living room
3 Dining room
4 Library
5 Master bedroom
6 Family room
7 Children's play area
8 Kitchen
9 Office
10 Secretary's room
11 Maid's room
12 Water feature
13 Turf
14 Laundry
15 Garage
16 Guard's room
17 Guest room
18 Massage room

0   5   10 metres

Opposite left Louvred timber screens protect the east-facing façade.

Opposite right The family pavilion that terminates the linear axis. The first floor is clad in timber with projecting 'monsoon' windows and a low-pitched overhanging roof.

Opposite below Ground floor plan.

Left Stone bridges span the dark linear pool that runs parallel to the *promenade architecturale*, connecting to the reception pavilion and the formal dining pavilion.

Below Deep overhangs shade the windows of the study.

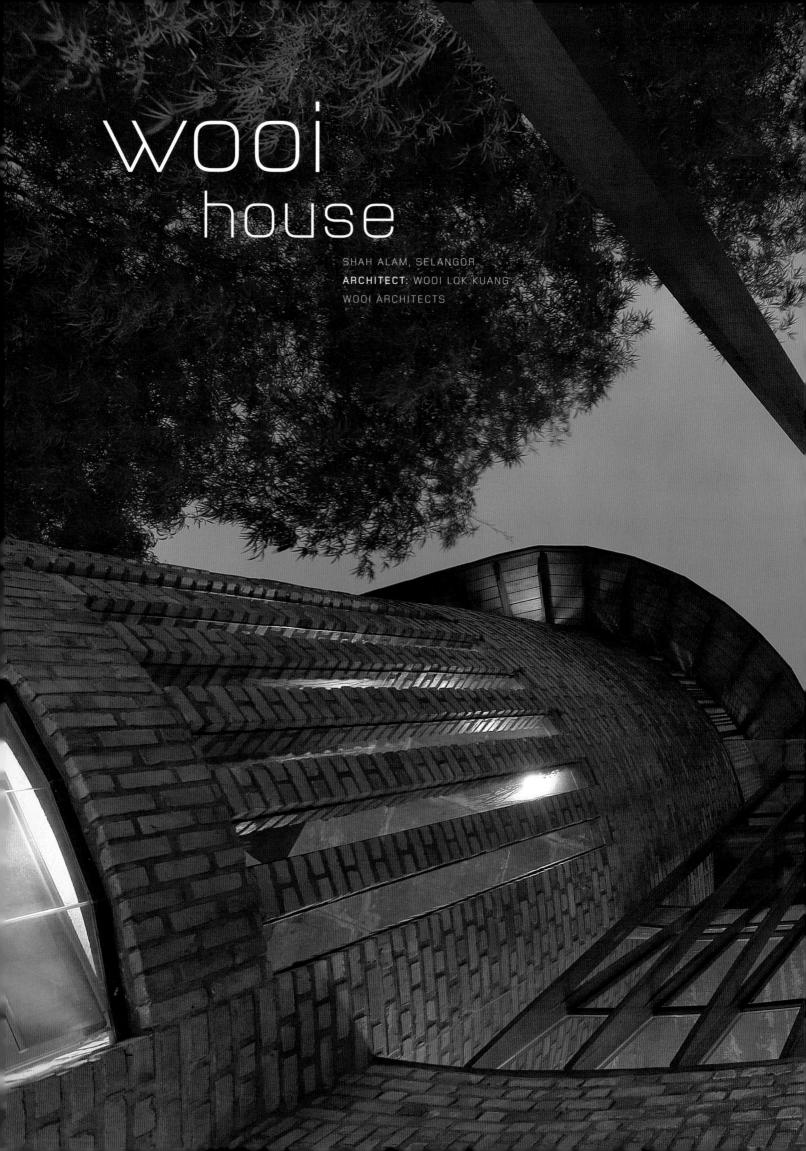

wooi
house

SHAH ALAM, SELANGOR
ARCHITECT: WOOI LOK KUANG
WOOI ARCHITECTS

Wooi Lok Kuang studied architecture at the University of New South Wales. His mentor during his final year was Russell Jack, a partner in Alan Jack and Cottier and designer of the Cater House. He also found inspiration in Bruce Rickard's Mirrabooka House and the houses of RAIA Gold Medal winner Rick Leplastrier, specifically the Rainforest House at Mapleton and Leplastrier's own house at Pittwater. The latter is a model of ecologically responsive design with respect for nature and the site.

Wooi lived in Sydney for ten years, and on his return to Malaysia in 1991 he took up employment with Jimmy CS Lim (also an alumnus of the University of New South Wales), where he was immediately involved in the detailing of the Schnyder House. Later he was project architect on the Impiana Resort Cherating in Pahang and spent some considerable time researching traditional architecture in Malaysia.

In 1996 Wooi quit CSL Architects to set up his own practice. The Wooi House, designed for his own family, is a succinct statement of his evolving architectural philosophy. It has enabled him to make connections with and evoke memories of his boyhood spent in a *kampung* (village) at Tanah Merah in Kedah.

The starting point for the construction of the house was the positioning of the main 16-metre-high structural column. This is closely connected with the ritual of building a *kampung* house where a *tiang seri* (principal post) is first placed on the selected site. From this column umbrella-like timber roof members in the shape of a fan radiate outwards and support a zinc titanium roof. Both plan and section are designed to ensure that no direct sunlight enters the main rooms.

The house is beguiling. Wooi insists that the sinuous plan form, in the shape of a crescent with a leaf-like protrusion, is not contrived, that it is simply a rational response to the topography and the limited views and has no covert symbolism.

Pages 48–9 A towering column, analogous with the *tiang seri* or principal post of a traditional Malay *kampung* house, is at the heart of the Wooi House.

Left Wide overhanging eaves, projecting timber floor joists and timber louvres attest to the lasting value of traditional joinery details.

Above In the master bedroom is an extraordinarily beautiful timber vaulted ceiling in the shape of a leaf.

The fair-faced brick aesthetic is closely related to Jimmy CS Lim's architectural language. Common bricks are used but wide joints make up for the inconsistencies and irregular sizes and give the walls an incredibly tactile quality. The bricks are slightly underburnt, which adds to the texture. There are reminders too of Laurie Baker's organic brick buildings at Trivandrum in southern India, but the Wooi House is more precise in its execution.

Careful detailing was necessary to ensure all services were installed accurately. To avoid chasing of the brickwork, the electrician had to work very closely with the bricklayer. Plastering of fair-faced brick walls was not an option and exposed conduits were ruled out. The cantilevered main staircase is aligned precisely with brick joints. Timber louvres filter light across the polished cement floors, imparting a slightly austere ambience.

The house is entered at ground level, 1.2 metres above the vehicle court. The entrance, on the north façade, leads into the curved reception room overlooking the bamboo-fringed courtyard on the south side of the house. A semicircular guest suite is located at the eastern extremity of the plan and the kitchen is situated at the western end, with the leaf-shaped dining room beyond, pointing southwest. A small balcony, a delightful place for a relaxed breakfast, cantilevers from the kitchen above the dark infinity pool on the western boundary.

Although Wooi has an office in the city, he frequently works from home. Here, his office is located at lower ground floor level overlooking the pool. It can be accessed from within the house or via an external stair from the vehicle court. Both the lower ground floor and ground floor have high ceilings, which aids cross-ventilation and cooling.

The first floor is the most private area of the house and contains a curved family room, the children's study area, two curved bedrooms and the *pièce de résistance*, the master bedroom, with an extraordinarily beautiful vaulted timber ceiling in the shape of a leaf.

Expressing his admiration for the work of the Swedish modernist Sigurd Lewerenz, who used brick in a contemporary manner, and for the tactile and sensory qualities of space in the work of Swiss architect Peter Zumthor, Wooi speaks of his own preoccupation with materiality, light and space when designing his house. He points out, with unconcealed delight, 'the sense of mystery in the curve' and how space is 'slowly revealed'. Enthusing about 'the architecture of the brick wall', he poetically defines the interior of the house as 'shades of darkness'.

Left The umbrella-like roof is supported on angled timber struts that radiate from the main structural column.

Below left Lower ground floor plan.

Below Evening sunlight filters across the timber floor in the children's study.

Right The courtyard faces south and is shaded by a bamboo grove. Dappled sunlight falls on the stone and gravel floor.

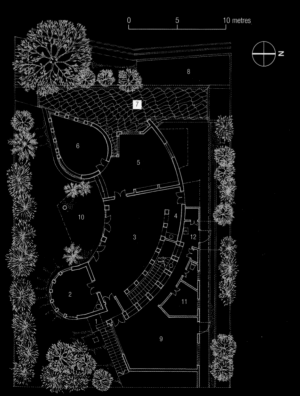

0   5   10 metres

Key
1 Lower entrance
2 Reception
3 Entertainment area
4 Bar
5 Library
6 Home office
7 Pool
8 Deck
9 Workshop
10 Patio
11 Utility room
12 Laundry

Key
3 Entertainment area
9 Workshop
10 Patio
13 Carport
14 Living room
15 Family room
16 Children's study deck

0   5   10 metres

Left The fan-shaped dining room flows through to the breakfast bar and kitchen beyond.

Opposite below left The master bedroom in the southwest corner of the site is in close proximity to the tree canopy.

Opposite below right Low horizontal windows in the bathroom *ensuite* facilitate views out while bathing.

Above Section through the Wooi House.

Below left and right Wide mortar joints make up for the inconsistencies and irregular sizes of the bricks and give the walls an exceptionally tactile quality.

Left At dusk, as lights are turned on, the south-facing courtyard takes on a mellow glow.

Right The meticulously fashioned junction of stair treads, the careful positioning of artefacts and the rigorously resolved brickwork junctions are evidence of the designer's keen eye for detail.

Below The architect refers poetically to the quality of light in the house as 'shades of darkness'.

sadeesh house

SUBANG JAYA, KUALA LUMPUR
ARCHITECT: ERNESTO BEDMAR
BEDMAR AND SHI

Pages 58–9 Three pavilions embrace the north-facing soft-landscaped central courtyard.

Left A rear verandah overlooks an azure blue swimming pool and distant views of the hills surrounding Kuala Lumpur.

Right The gentle murmur of a fountain and the refection of light on fish scales animate the water court alongside the dining area.

A graduate of the University of Architecture and Planning at Cordoba in Argentina, Ernesto Bedmar arrived in Singapore in 1984 via Hong Kong where he worked in the office of his compatriot Miguel Angel Roca.

Three years after coming to Singapore, Bedmar and interior designer Patsy Shi founded Bedmar and Shi Designers (now Bedmar and Shi Pte Ltd), and since then Bedmar has been in the forefront of residential design in Southeast Asia. He has acquired a reputation for architecture of understated elegance and sophistication and his tranquil dwellings and interiors have been widely published.

The Sadeesh House is entered through an enclosed vehicle court and then, on a primary axis, through a tall, pivoted timber door that is an instant reminder of the entrance to the Villa Sarabhai in Ahmedabad designed by Le Corbusier (1951). This is uncanny, for Smita Sadeesh hails from Gujarat and she is related to the Sarabhai family. The main axis through the house terminates with an artefact from Kerala, a ship's prow, that evokes memories of the southernmost state in India and the origin of the family of Sadeesh Ragavan. Bedmar has always exhibited a remarkable ability to subtly condense memories within a dwelling. One of his earliest designs was the seminal Eu House in Singapore (1993), which is often credited with changing the direction of residential design in the city-state.

Proceeding into the Sadeesh House there is a heightened sense of calm that precedes a gently choreographed journey through a variety of carefully orchestrated spaces.

The plan of the house is essentially three pavilions attached to the primary axis – an open-sided verandah that is orientated almost west to east. The pavilions embrace a north-facing soft-landscaped courtyard and each pavilion has a separate monopitch roof sloping towards the courtyard.

The first single-storey pavilion encountered upon entering the house contains a guest suite with a bathroom *ensuite* and a tiny open-to-sky walled garden. The second pavilion, also single storey, at the end of the axis, is taller and glazed on three sides. This is the living area and the principal space for entertaining friends. It looks west into the garden court and east, beyond a screen of banana palms and frangipani trees, to the distant hills. Beyond the living room is an external verandah overlooking a swimming pool that has the appearance of a bejewelled fragment of the Malabar Coast uplifted and dropped into the lower terrace.

The south side of the axis is defined by a substantial wall of uncoursed stone that effectively screens the more private areas of the house from those most accessible to visitors. The largest pavilion, a two-storey structure, is located immediately to the south and parallel with the wall. The wall excludes entry to the first-floor bedrooms and at ground floor conceals the wet and dry kitchens, the laundry and the maid's rooms. A linear pond, dramatically lit by filtered sunlight, runs parallel to the stone wall. A horizontal opening in the wall creates a visual link to the formal dining area that overlooks a water court pervaded by the gentle murmur of a fountain. At subbasement level is an extensive library, a study and an audio-visual room with views to the pool deck.

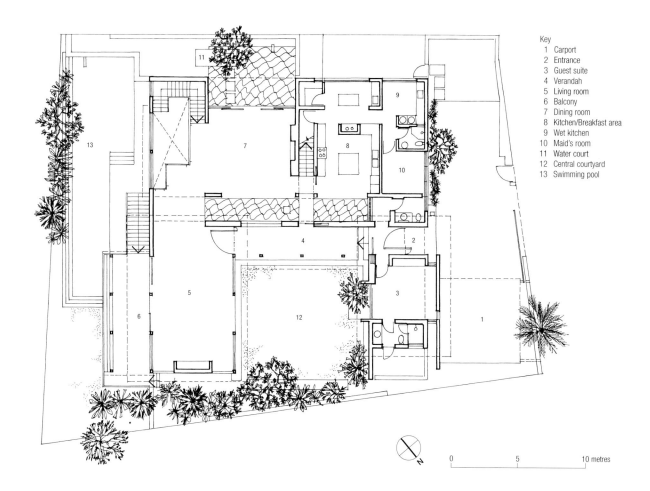

Key
1 Carport
2 Entrance
3 Guest suite
4 Verandah
5 Living room
6 Balcony
7 Dining room
8 Kitchen/Breakfast area
9 Wet kitchen
10 Maid's room
11 Water court
12 Central courtyard
13 Swimming pool

0   5   10 metres

The modern language of the house, with its free-form plan, white planar walls and zincalume monopitched roofs, is effectively balanced by the abundance of stone, timber columns, pergolas, projecting windows, louvres and traditional details that draw upon the clients' cultural memory: a timber *jali* in the form of a sliding security screen at the head of the stairs, a carved timber light fitting above the dining table in the form of a nine-square *mandala*, carved columns from Bangalore and numerous clay pots and stone carvings from the Indian subcontinent.

The joy of this house is in the vertical and horizontal movement through space, the countless 'surprises' along the route, the unexpected niches and secluded places for quiet contemplation, the reflections in placid dark ponds, the strategically placed vantage points, the unanticipated breezes, the interplay of roof forms, the penetration of light through a pergola, the sensuous ripple of waves on the pool, the stepping stones and, ultimately, the kaleido-scopic effect of all these events. This is truly architecture of the senses.

The notion of karma is deeply embedded in Hindu philosophy and can relate to the atmosphere radiated by a place, a situation or an object. The Sadeesh House is a poetic design solution arising out of a response to site, climate and a dialogue between global and local culture. The house has an intangible quality, a spirit that is soothing and at the same time enchanting.

Above left Ground floor plan.

Above White planar walls and zincalume monopitched roofs typify the modern language of the house.

Left The primary axis terminates with an artefact from Kerala – a ship's prow. The open-sided verandah leads to the living room.

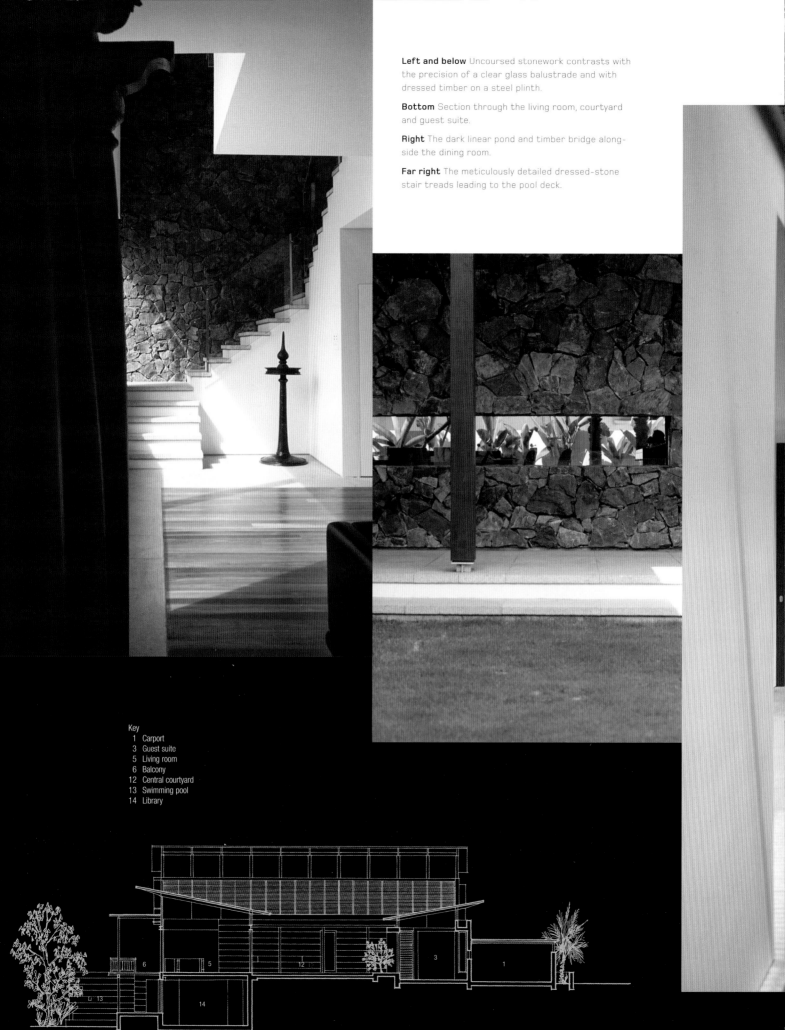

Left and below Uncoursed stonework contrasts with the precision of a clear glass balustrade and with dressed timber on a steel plinth.

Bottom Section through the living room, courtyard and guest suite.

Right The dark linear pond and timber bridge alongside the dining room.

Far right The meticulously detailed dressed-stone stair treads leading to the pool deck.

Key
1 Carport
3 Guest suite
5 Living room
6 Balcony
12 Central courtyard
13 Swimming pool
14 Library

safari roofhouse

DAMANSARA INDAH, KUALA LUMPUR
ARCHITECT: KEVIN LOW
SMALLPROJECTS

'smallprojects is characterized by an entirely uncorporate identity, ironically grown from eleven years of corporate history. It is less concerned about the theatrical than it is about the dramatic. It has more to do with possibility than it does with statement. It is about subverting the dominant paradigm.' KEVIN LOW

Kevin Low's smallprojects is a one-man practice and that is the way he wants it to remain. A graduate of the University of Oregon and Massachusetts Institute of Technology, Low set up his practice in 2002 in order 'to reclaim old dreams'. Prior to that, he worked with Kamil Merican in the multi-disciplinary firm of GDP Architects.

Low is totally focused on what he wants to achieve in architecture. He abhors the fetishing of buildings, the divorce from context, the idea of architecture as 'object rather than process'. He also dislikes the idea of boundary fences, preferring houses to interact with the public domain, and for there to be an area of ambiguity between public and private spaces.

Low also likes 'down-to-earth' and 'found' materials. He is fascinated by tactile surfaces – handmade bricks which age gradually and concrete that acquires a mantle of moss and climbing plants. He likes 'unfinished' modern architecture that readily accepts, in the manner of Carlo Scarpa's Tomb of Brion Vega or Geoffrey Bawa's Kandalama Hotel, a patina of age. He is particularly inspired by the British artist Andy Goldsworthy and his use of contextual materials – allowing artistic works to age and revert to nature. Goldsworthy

regards all his creations as transient or ephemeral. He generally works with whatever comes to hand. This is an idea that infiltrates Low's architectural process.

But the initial inspiration for the Safari Roof House came from an unconventional source – the design of a modified British Land Rover that had a 'sun breaker' roof, a second canopy with an air gap to promote ventilation and cooling of the interior that was referred to as a safari roof. The roof of the Safari Roof House is consequently constructed in corrugated 'ondoline' floating above a concrete slab.

In common with other dwellings designed by Low, the Safari Roof House concept sketches focus upon a large 'garden room'. In this case, the outdoor room is manifested as a rectangular court with a shimmering lap pool, a linear grove of 36 tall slender trees (*Tristania*, *Koompassia excelsa*, *Hopea odurata*, *Eugenia lace* and *Pelong*) casting dappled shadows and a framed view to the south over a golf course. There is duality in the house plan: the west-facing entrance elevation

Pages 66–7 At the core of the house is a garden 'room', an expansive courtyard with a grove of slender trees and a shimmering blue lap pool.

Opposite The route from the compressed space of the entrance to the expansive courtyard reveals the architect as a master of spatial choreography.

Above The garden 'room' is fringed by dense vegetation that frames the view to the south over a golf course.

is relatively closed, with small window openings, whereas the eastern façade is open, with larger windows looking towards the golf course.

The house is designed with primary concern for the interior. The exterior is not seen from any vantage point, nor is it visible to the outsider, and thus its appearance is considered to be of less importance. The principal material employed in the construction is Ventblock, a 200 mm x 200 mm precast concrete block normally used for walls that are subsequently plastered. But here it is simultaneously used as decoration, as texture, as porous sun filter and as detached screens overgrown with *Ficus pumila*. Floors are generally polished cement. Low describes Japanese concrete as 'pedigree concrete' and his own concrete as 'dog concrete' because there is a certain roughness to it. Low considers the way a building will age is critical; it is important to consider where moss and algae growth will occur so the house is designed to age well under the combined influence of sun and rain. The designer describes the house as 'a reconciliation between modernism, context, culture and the influence of the ageing process'.

Low's is a vigorous critique of Malaysian architecture. He speaks out vehemently against the picturesque and rejects minimalism, which he dismisses as 'neo-clinical' architecture. His own houses are a mixture of austerity and delight in equal measure. The route from the compressed space of the entrance lobby via a 90-degree turn to the open verandah and thence to the outdoor room and a dining table by the pool reveals Low as a master of spatial choreography. The juxtaposition of the four 'pavilions' that form the plan of the house channels breezes and aids natural ventilation.

There is a confident grasp of spatial composition in the double-height living room, a space that is transformed in the evening as the setting sun turns the western louvred wall into a filigree of light. There is delight also in details such as the sliding-folding entrance gate, the 3-metre-high pivoted entrance door and the thin floating roof planes carried on slender circular columns.

The Safari Roof House is magical as night falls. A light breeze springs up, candles and up-lighters are lit and the outdoor room becomes a haven of calm and conviviality.

Key
1 Entrance
2 Living room
4 Garden court
12 Lap pool

0   5   10 metres

Opposite above left Detached concrete block walls are overgrown with *Ficus pumila* that softens the outline of the modernist architecture.

Opposite above right As night falls the garden room becomes a haven of calm and the location for evening parties by the pool.

Top Section through the garden room.

Left The house is a mixture of austerity and delight in equal measure.

Above The inspiration for the floating roof came from a modified British Land Rover that incorporated a second skin with an air gap to facilitate ventilation.

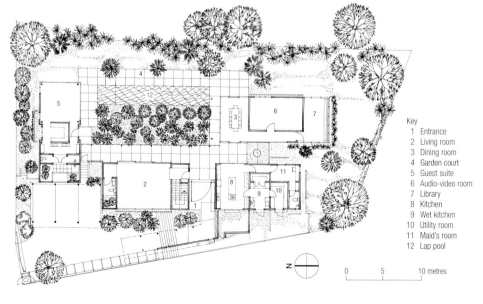

Key
1 Entrance
2 Living room
3 Dining room
4 Garden court
5 Guest suite
6 Audio-video room
7 Library
8 Kitchen
9 Wet kitchen
10 Utility room
11 Maid's room
12 Lap pool

z

0   5   10 metres

Above The setting sun transforms the wall of the double-height living room into a filigree of light.

Far left Trees in the courtyard are carefully selected with slender trunks to provide shade while permitting uninterrupted views to the south.

Left Ground floor plan.

Right Robust materials – concrete blocks, handmade bricks and zinc roof sheets – are juxtaposed to stunning effect.

caracol
house

KUALA LUMPUR
ARCHITECTS: FRANK LING & PILAR GONZALEZ-HERRAIZ
ARCHITRON DESIGN CONSULTANTS

'Our work has always been related to the intrinsic needs and enjoyment of the user. This involves much "interrogation" and dialogue to bring about self-realization [by the clients] of what are their true "needs" and what is bias and prejudice – driven by populism, lifestyle mongers and the media. These physical and psychological "needs" take precedence in the programme for a home; not ready-made needs imposed by us, or preconceived style.' FRANK LING

Architron is a design practice of a husband and wife team who operate from offices in Kuala Lumpur and Madrid. Sarawak-born Frank Ling and Spanish-born Pilar Gonzalez-Herraiz are both graduates of the AA School of Architecture in London. Ling also holds a Masters degree from RMIT in Melbourne. Prior to setting up their design practice in 1994, Gonzalez-Herraiz worked with Alison and Peter Smithson, Arup Associates and briefly with Jimmy CS Lim while Ling gained experience with Nicholas Grimshaw, Ron Herron and Hijjas Kasturi. Both worked in London for almost a decade in the 1980s and 1990s. This breadth of experience underpins their work.

They also share a common appreciation of the modernist architect Hans Scharoun (1893–1972) because, as Ling explains, 'at the height of the modern movement his architecture was different; very organic. His offsets, fragmented orientations, sequences and special responses were each distinct and yet there was a strong underlying continuity. His architecture revealed a defiance and irony aimed at the [political] regime within which he worked.'

The design of the Caracol House employs filmic techniques in that the journey through the house is not a simple linear sequence but is composed of long shots and close-ups, panoramic and zooming views, static and dynamic 'flashbacks', fast-forward sequences, tightly composed scenes and unexpected surprises. These techniques are not dissimilar to those used by an urban designer who manipulates space using, for example, spatial compression, expansion and termination, anticipation, deflection as well as various changes of levels, gradients and materials to regulate speed. It is not surprising that both Ling and Gonzalez-Herraiz have an affinity with the movies of Fellini, Altman and Tarkovsky. They allude to 'Tarkovsky's mental and phenomenal spaces, memories and actions' and 'the multiple characters and plots' of Fellini and Altman 'that are so real and tangible and earthy'.

Pages 74–5 The house takes the form of a south-facing U shape that embraces and protects the occupants.

Left The interplay of space, light and dramatic colours is the distinguishing feature of the house.

Above Limited external vistas dictated an inward-orientated dwelling that focuses on spatial experience.

Right Ground floor plan.

Key
5 Swimming pool
6 Living room
7 Kitchen/Breakfast area
8 Dining room
9 Audio-visual room
10 Covered terrace
11 Open terrace
12 Raised terrace
13 Wet kitchen/Storeroom
14 Utility room
15 Maid's room

The name Caracol, meaning 'snail' in Spanish, is appropriate, for conceptually the design of this house is a helix, a spiral form that defines movement. Essentially, the plan is a southwest-facing U shape that forms a protective 'shell', capped by a soaring roof that embraces and shelters the occupants.

Entering the rectangular house compound from the southwest corner, a short driveway in the form of a quadrant leads to the entrance porch located in the subbasement. Immediately to the left of the entrance is a line of rectangular portholes puncturing the wall of the swimming pool. They appear as shimmering azure blue 'lenses', and occasionally bodies can be seen beneath the water surface. Children in goggles delight in pulling faces at surprised visitors. This is one example of the fast-forward technique, giving a preview of experiences to come.

Wheeling sharply left in the entrance lobby, a diverging corridor ascends via a series of shallow risers to the 'crossroads' at the heart of the house; to the left is the living room and, turning a full 180 degrees, an open terrace parallel to the swimming pool glimpsed earlier. Beyond the pool a raised timber deck shields the private activities of the household from neighbouring dwellings. Security and privacy are deeply embedded in the design concept.

A 180-degree turn to the right at the crossroads leads to the dining space and breakfast area and another long shallow staircase, beckoning upwards between walls to the first floor. Arriving at a half landing, a final 180-degree turn signals the start of a shallow ramp leading to the master bedroom suite.

There are few external views to exploit in this essentially urban location and the house focuses inwards to the pool and the deck, which become an extension of the living area. The master bedroom, study and activity room are similarly orientated towards this external space.

Seemingly random placed windows facing the pool deck are of a variety of sizes and their reveals are painted in a multitude of pigments so that the light entering the house through these apertures is tinged with multiple hues and shades. Continuing the cinematographic analogy, the windows are like movie 'stills' framing views of the outside world. All the paints were specially mixed for the house; a palette of twenty-five colours appear to change like a kaleidoscope in different external lighting conditions. This interplay of light, space and the interpenetration of space is the distinguishing feature of the house interior. Strategically placed paintings and furniture enhance the spatial experience.

The making of the Caracol House involved spontaneous and multidirectional negotiations as part of the rigorous process to distil the client's needs. The end result is a flexible, open-ended, spontaneous and responsive environment intended 'to nurture self and place awareness' and ultimately to provide pleasure.

Top There is a dramatic introduction to the house with underwater views of the swimming pool from the entrance porch.

Above Space is skilfully manipulated to conjure up tightly composed sequences and unanticipated surprises.

Right The staircase ascends gently to the upper floors while the third riser returns as a bench seat in the dining room.

Above The house has a dramatic soaring roof. Seemingly random placed windows facing the pool deck are of a variety of shapes and sizes.

Left Section through the living room and pool deck.

Above right The swimming pool is shielded from the view of neighbouring houses by a raised timber deck and dense planting.

Right The pool and the timber deck are an outdoor extension of the living area.

0   5   10 metres

Key
2 Porch
5 Swimming pool
6 Living room
12 Raised terrace
16 Study

Lydia's house

KOTA DAMANSARA, KUALA LUMPUR
ARCHITECTS: DAVID CHAN WENG CHEONG & CHAN MUN INN
DCA (DESIGN COLLECTIVE ARCHITECTURE NETWORK)

Lydia's House has a presence that far exceeds its modest size. Located on a flat suburban lot surrounded by burgeoning residential development, the house is essentially an orthogonal composition of planes and voids resulting in a sculptural form that differentiates it from its more conventional neighbours.

Because of its suburban location, the architects have concentrated on creating a private domain. At the heart of the flat-roofed dwelling is an open-to-sky landscaped courtyard while the living room and master bedroom enjoy 'framed' views of the Sungai Buloh Forest Reserve situated to the north.

The upper floor of the two-storey unit projects one metre beyond the ground floor, with window openings 'carved out' of the white cubist form. The principal façade reads as a white portal framing the living room and adjacent carport.

A triangular swimming pool is slotted into a residual slice of land on the eastern flank of the house.

David Chan Weng Cheong and Chan Mun Inn, the partners in DCA (Design Collective Architecture Network), both studied architecture at the School of Architecture, Construction and Planning, Curtin University of Technology in Western Australia where they were introduced to environmental science and appropriate technology by Associate Professor Neville D'Cruz. Headed by Professor Laurie Hegvold, there was a strong emphasis at the School on sustainable architecture and passive solar design.[1] When they returned to Malaysia, David Chan worked with Jimmy CS Lim and Chan Mun Inn with Peter Ho prior to setting up DCA.

Equally influential was their admiration of Le Corbusier, Rudolf Schindler and Marcel Breuer, and the influence of these renowned figures is evident in the architectural

language of Lydia's House with its reductive form, emphasis on interlocking volumes and planar surfaces, and the absence of decorative elements. Yet DCA's modernism is tempered by their response to the equatorial climate of Kuala Lumpur, which demands deep-set recesses, shading of windows, cross-ventilation and orientation related to the sun path and predominant breezes.

The two partners are fascinated by the process of architecture and how architecture is 'made'. Consequently, their projects progress through numerous physical models utilizing the traditional tools of the architectural model maker – white card and compressed polystyrene – before being transferred to computers for production of construction documents.

[1] Professor Laurie Hegvold subsequently became Pro-Vice Chancellor of the Sarawak campus of the Curtin University of Technology.

Pages 82–3 The house is a sculptural composition of planar surfaces and interlocking voids influenced by the pioneers of the modern movement.

Above The dining space with breakfast area beyond. The open-plan house is a model for compact urban living.

Right At the very core of the house is a landscaped courtyard.

Left Family life revolves around the garden courtyard that brings life into the centre of the dwelling and assists in cross-ventilation.

Above and right Crisp detailing and a limited palette of white painted walls and black window frames are reflected in the triangle-shaped swimming pool.

Above The architects respond to the tropical climate with deep window reveals.

Right A low horizontal window gives views out to the carport.

Opposite above left Ground floor plan.

Opposite above right Modern prints and paintings enhance the planar white walls.

Opposite below A white concrete portal frame spans the living room and adjacent carport.

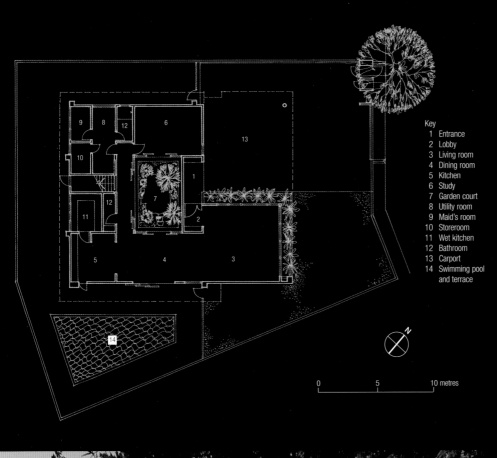

Key
1 Entrance
2 Lobby
3 Living room
4 Dining room
5 Kitchen
6 Study
7 Garden court
8 Utility room
9 Maid's room
10 Storeroom
11 Wet kitchen
12 Bathroom
13 Carport
14 Swimming pool
and terrace

0   5   10 metres

extended family houses

ambi house

NILAI, SEREMBAN
ARCHITECTS: DAVID CHAN WENG CHEONG & CHAN MUN INN
DCA (DESIGN COLLECTIVE ARCHITECTURE NETWORK)

The built work of Le Corbusier, Rudolf Schindler and Marcel Breuer has been influential in the development of David Chan Weng Cheong and Chan Mun Inn's architecture. They credit the modernist pioneers with giving them insights into structural clarity and three-dimensional creation of space. They have also grown to appreciate the architecture of Tadao Ando and his exploitation of positive and negative space, and this too finds its way into their work. Unusual in today's computer-driven design culture, the two partners in DCA prefer to work towards design solutions through numerous physical models. Planar surfaces typify their oeuvre, juxtaposed against strong horizontal lines, over-sized louvres and heavy shading.

The Ambi House is the result of an unusual brief. The house is for an extended family of painters and creative writers comprising eight adults and two teenagers. The adults are siblings. Each 'branch' of the family formerly lived in sepa-rate dwellings but decided they could collaborate more effectively if they were to reside under one roof and pool resources as a single household. A sloping site was acquired on the edge of a rubber plantation.

Pages 90–1 The four identical villas at the multigenerational Johor House complex (page 112).

Pages 92–3 The Ambi House is located on sloping ground on the fringe of a rubber estate.

Left The upper floor is ex-pressed as a timber box float-ing above a white masonry ground floor block.

Above Horizontal timber louvres ensure the house interior is shaded and cool.

Ambi Mathe, who provided a very detailed brief of the family requirements and cost constraints, is the second eldest of the eight brothers and sisters. In intensive workshop sessions involving members of the family and the architects, the design was quickly conceptualized.

Essentially, the two-storey house comprises a 27-metre-long, 8-metre-wide rectangular block. The first floor is expressed as a linear box clad with *kempas* wood, slightly offset above a heavier and grounded white-rendered masonry ground floor. The house is located on a hillside and traverses the contours before cantilevering out over a stone retaining wall at the northern extremity. Access to the house is from the lowest level of the site via a stair-case on the eastern flank.

The ground-floor accommodation consists of a high-ceilinged room, 17 metres long and 6 metres wide, embrac-ing living and dining spaces and communal activities. A separate TV room and wet and dry kitchens complete the accommodation, along with a utility room accessed from the upper level of the site. The large communal room has sliding louvred screens on both long façades and opens out to a garden on the western flank.

The first-floor plan is equally uncomplicated; six family bedrooms are arranged along the western flank of the house, with a guest room located in the southeast corner. A single-loaded corridor affords access to all rooms. All seven bedrooms in the house are of similar size except that two rooms have individual bathrooms whereas the remainder have twin-sharing arrangements.

The internal finishes are inexpensive and hard-wearing – polished cement on the ground floor and local hardwood timber on the first floor. The house relies on natural ventilation although air conditioning is provided for occasions when there are many guests in the house. The owners enjoy a 'rustic' lifestyle and there are many plants within the shared house.

The site configuration and underlying geology have determined some compromises with regard to the orientation of the house in response to the sun path, but the overall impression is of a modern design driven by functional imperatives. The interior exhibits unambiguous planning and spatial clarity while the external form has a distinct sculptural quality befitting a house for an extended family of creative artists.

Left A sheltered verandah gives access to the bedrooms arranged in a linear manner on the upper floor.

Above The principal space is a tall
17-metre-long communal living
and dining room. The efficient
cross-ventilation is evident.

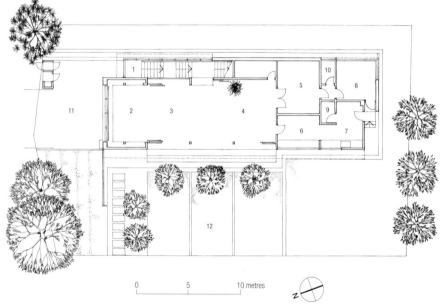

Above Sliding louvred screens open out to the west-facing garden. The garden is an extension of the interior space.

Left and below Ground floor plan and elevation.

Above right The north façade cantilevers over a random-rubble stone wall.

Right The strong linear form of the house contrasts with the natural environment.

0   5   10 metres

Key
1   Entrance
2   Living room
3   Communal area
4   Dining room
5   TV room
6   Dry kitchen
7   Wet kitchen
8   Utility room
9   Storeroom
10 Toilet
11 Forecourt/Parking
12 Garden

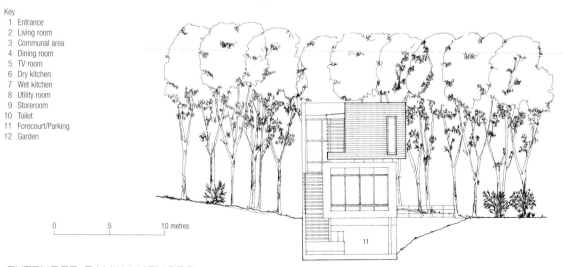

0   5   10 metres

tierra house

LAKEVIEW BUNGALOWS, SAUJANA RESORT, SHAH ALAM
ARCHITECTS: FRANK LING & PILAR GONZALEZ-HERRAIZ
ARCHITRON DESIGN CONSULTANTS

Pages 100–1 The Tierra House has a striking roof form consisting of overlapping copper-surfaced corrugated sheets supported on 10-metre-high columns.

Above The focus of the house is a spacious south-facing outdoor room. It is an intimate private patio yet it has the ambience of an urban plaza.

Opposite The bedrooms are designed as independent modules overlooking the plaza.

'Style is not our preoccupation or our concern. It emerges as a consequence of the design process. The architecture is totally process driven. This is a custom-built house, tailored to the intrinsic needs and enjoyment of the family.'
FRANK LING & PILAR GONZALEZ-HERRAIZ

The Tierra House is designed for a large extended family with regular visiting relatives, and it was necessary to understand the dynamics involved. The architects, Frank Ling and Pilar Gonzalez-Herraiz, the husband and wife team who head Architron Design Consultants, analysed the life-style and living patterns of the client's family to discern their real needs. In the process, they attempted to subdue their own preferences in terms of form and language and allowed the form to emerge from the dialogue with the client and the distillation of opportunities from specific site and climatic conditions. They jointly explored and discovered a new architectural vocabulary.

The fragmented arrangement of rooms appears at first to be the result of deconstruction theory, but the designers affirm that nothing could be further from the truth. The house is the result of working with the site, the sun, the wind and, most importantly, the client. 'The architecture is process driven,' asserts Ling, 'a process that involves extensive dissection, reflection and negotiation to achieve equilibrium.'

The focus of the house is a stunning courtyard, a spacious two-storey south-facing 'outdoor room' which forms an in-between space with unique qualities. It has the intimacy and privacy of a domestic patio yet simultaneously displays the ambience of an urban plaza to embody a distinct spatial hierarchy. The plaza is divided into 'public' space (the entrance terrace) linked by a bridge to an inner more 'private' terrace. A channel of water, akin to a 'stream', springs from a fountain, tumbles over a weir and flows beneath the bridge into an azure blue pool. A grand stair-case flies dramatically over the pool in the manner of a Chinese bridge pavilion.

The principal spaces at ground-floor level – the living room, family room, gym and dining/kitchen – are designed as independent modules encircling the 'plaza'. The three boys' rooms and the master bedroom at first floor level also appear as separate units overlooking the communal space, while the grandparent's suite is separate yet visually connected to the terrace. The plan can also be read in terms of the growing independence of three teenage sons against a backdrop of continuous interaction of an extended family.

Right The children's bedrooms are articulated as three identical but independent boxes.

Below A channel of water springs from a small fountain and tumbles over a weir alongside the patio.

Above A grand staircase rises over the swimming pool to the master bedroom.

Right The metal roof is supported on slender circular steel columns.

Above The outdoor space can be read as a 'stage' for the private enactment of unscripted family life.

Right The family room overlooks the gymnasium and the bridge over the swimming pool.

Initially the plan was orthogonal in response to the rectilinear site configuration, but sight lines were added orien-
tating rooms to identified vistas, and then the plan was
adjusted in response to wind, sunlight and *feng shui*. Each
and every adjustment impacted on the design and neces-
sitated further adjustments so that the plan was developed
holistically.

As the house has to deal with humidity, the client required
efficient natural ventilation and as much daylight as possible. Taken together, these factors determined the final
form. A clear duality emerged, the porosity of the south-
facing façade contrasting with the 'fortified' perimeter
wall on the other three sides. The plan is disaggregated
to encourage cross-ventilation, while the gaps between
the various elements encourage the ingress of breezes.
The dynamic roof form consists of overlapping copper-
surfaced profiled steel planes angled in response to the
sun and rain. Supported on 10-metre-high slender tilting
circular-section steel columns, the roof is analogous with
the rainforest canopy, providing shade, filtering the sun and
deflecting the rain.

Ling emphasizes that this is an 'equatorial' house reflecting
the reality that the house is located three degrees north
of the equator. Any house in this latitude has to contend
with seasonal variation in the direction of the sun, which
shifts from the northern hemisphere to the southern
hemisphere as the earth flips on its axis.

Yet another reading of the house is that it is a 'stage' upon
which the multiplicity of family life is privately enacted with
an ever-evolving script. The central space comes to life
when animated by family and friends seated around the
'café' table or around the edge of the pool. Music can be
relayed to the outdoor spaces from a central console.
Light springs from natural and artificial sources and is
directed, diffused and reflected onto a variety of coloured
surfaces. The hues and shades are drawn from nature, with
a profusion of yellows, greens, oranges, reds and blues.

The use of the Spanish word 'tierra' to describe the house
encompasses multiple interpretations, from the poetic
sense of one's own 'private earth/world' to open space and
domain, to terrain and topography and cultural landscape.
The multiplicity of meanings of the word 'tierra' and their
relationship was very much part of the architects' design
process and it articulates the many levels that create the
individual's own world.

In October 2007, Architron Design Consultants was awarded the Gold Medal of the World Association of Chinese
Architects (WACA) for the design of the Tierra House.

Above The staircase spans the
swimming pool in the manner
of a Chinese bridge pavilion.

Left Open windows alongside the pool direct breezes into the living room when air conditioning is not in use.

Below The 'earthy' palette of colours employed throughout the house is drawn from nature.

Right The stunning entrance to the living room from the patio.

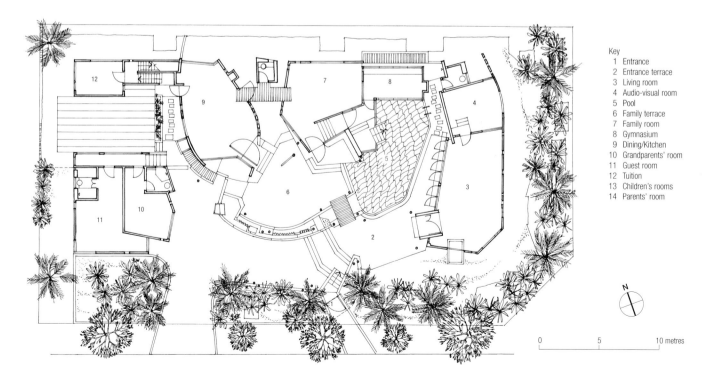

Key
1 Entrance
2 Entrance terrace
3 Living room
4 Audio-visual room
5 Pool
6 Family terrace
7 Family room
8 Gymnasium
9 Dining/Kitchen
10 Grandparents' room
11 Guest room
12 Tuition
13 Children's rooms
14 Parents' room

0   5   10 metres

Left The vehicular entrance to the house clearly demarcates the transition from the public to the private domain.

Below left Ground floor plan.

Above Section through the house.

Right and below A collage of details: the pedestrian entrance to the house; the portico framing the door to the living room, and the roof above the plaza that provides shade and filters the sun.

0   5   10 metres

13   13   13

6

5   4

johor house

LEISURE FARM RESORT, JOHOR
ARCHITECTS: JOHN DING & KEN WONG
UNIT ONE DESIGN

The Johor House is a multigenerational family dwelling consisting of five separate but linked villas within a compound located close to what is referred to as 'the second crossing' between Malaysia and Singapore. The gently sloping site has few natural features but will eventually be planted with an orchard and trees around the perimeter. One dwelling is designated for the parents' occupation and for family gatherings, with semi-independent villas for each of their four children and their families.

At the outset of the design, architects John Ding and Ken Wong of Unit One Design sought to create a strong diagram. This is a strategy inspired by Kerry Hill for whom both partners express their admiration. In the Johor House this is expressed as a V-shaped plan with the apex pointing to the northeast and two 'wings' splayed at an acute angle to enclose a southeast-facing triangular garden. The longer of the two wings runs due east. Essentially, this is a 100-metre *promenade architecturale* to which the villas of the four siblings are attached like parallel ribs, that gradually descends some 7.5 metres at 15-metre intervals pointing south.

The four villas are of precisely the same configuration, with a master bedroom at first-floor level and an open-plan living/dining and kitchen at ground-floor level overlooking a south-facing timber deck sheltered by a 6-metre-high cantilevered roof. Three bedrooms at basement level look into a high walled private courtyard. Each house is orientated east and south so that it presents a less transparent façade to the west.

The shorter of the two wings runs south-southwest for slightly less than 50 metres, and arrayed along this route are various shared family spaces in the form of a library, a study and a games room overlooking a pool. Extending some 150 metres beyond the pool is a narrow walkway leading to a viewing tower in the southeast corner of the site.

At the apex of the two wings, on slightly higher ground, is the 'parents' house', which is similar in its linear form to the dwellings of their four children. All the rooms in the main house are orientated towards the east, and a wide terrace

looks across the garden metaphorically embracing and protecting the family. The formal entrance to the family compound is on the western boundary. The main house is the principal space for reunions of the immediate family members and their extended family from different parts of the world. A number of formal and informal reception and dining spaces are grouped around the foyer.

The architectural language of the Johor House is assertively modern, with shallow inclined roofs projecting over the semitransparent orthogonal boxes that comprise the accommodation. Materials are fair-faced concrete, powder-coated aluminium screens, tempered glass, pvdf2-coated steel standing seam roofs, coloured glass louvres and timber. There is throughout a controlled geometry that relates to the initial diagram.

The notion of an extended family compound is particularly relevant in Asian society and the brief for the house was formulated by a strong matriarchal figure. The plan of the house reflects a family structure that shares a strong bond but allows some freedom for each family member. The architectural language is unambiguously forward looking and innovative.

Below left, centre and right Shallow inclined roofs, exposed rolled steel joists (RSJ's), perforated aluminium louvres and aluminium-framed windows create a consistent vocabulary.

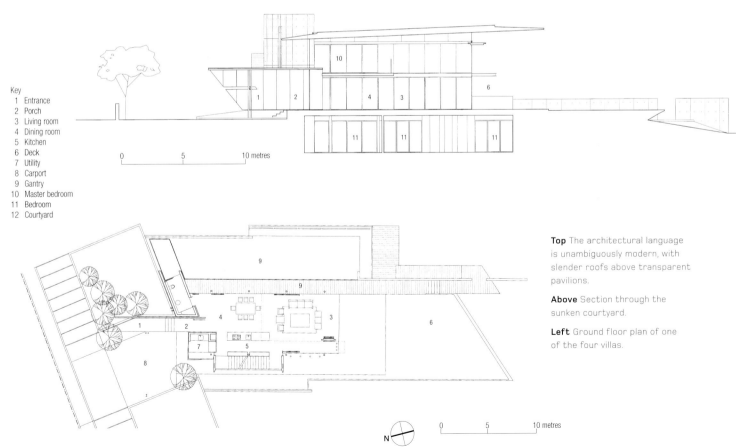

Key
1 Entrance
2 Porch
3 Living room
4 Dining room
5 Kitchen
6 Deck
7 Utility
8 Carport
9 Gantry
10 Master bedroom
11 Bedroom
12 Courtyard

0   5   10 metres

Top The architectural language is unambiguously modern, with slender roofs above transparent pavilions.

Above Section through the sunken courtyard.

Left Ground floor plan of one of the four villas.

N

0   5   10 metres

Left The master bedroom is located on a mezzanine level overlooking the living and dining space.

Above Double-height doors at the southern end of the living room fold aside and extend the interior out to the sheltered patio.

Above A 100-metre *promenade architecturale* links the
five dwellings to the parents' residence. Each house has
a double carport with steps up to an entrance verandah.

0 5 10 metres

N

Opposite left Plan of the family compound.

Opposite right Adjustable louvred screens filter the morning sun and ensure privacy.

Above Each house has a secure walled garden.

Left On the south side of each house is a stone and timber patio that extends to a garden with a triangular grass *padang* (field) in the centre of the site.

Right An informal route connects the four dwellings.

X1 house

SIERRAMAS, SUNGAI BULOH, SELANGOR
ARCHITECT: LIM TENG NGIOM
NGIOM PARTNERSHIP

Pages 124–5 A cantilevered vertical slab of grey lava rock forms a visual barrier in front of the main staircase in the Pixie House (page 160).

Pages 126–7 A pristine white composition of 'cubes of space', the X1 House cascades down a 29-degree slope at Sierramas.

Sierramas is one of a growing number of gated communities in Kuala Lumpur. The developer's guidelines stipulate that individual dwellings within Sierramas must exhibit openness to the street and that tall front boundary walls and iron entrance gates are not permitted. However, there are no stipulations on the style of architecture, and this has resulted in the juxtaposition of houses of widely differing sensitivities.

Xl House is a pristine white composition of 'cubes of space' designed in section to cascade five storeys down a 29-degree slope. The architect's intention was that the dwelling should hug the terrain rather than be raised on stilts. The rectangular footprint runs from southwest to northeast, with a dynamic roofline expressed as a series of monopitch roofs and a 'tower' thrusting vertically at the highest point.

The geometric composition clusters around an open-to-sky courtyard with a pond and a sitting area. The courtyard is the focus of the house, open on its northwest side and visually connected to the living room and dining area and overlooked by the family room. An external bridge and two flights of stairs also flank the space so that it is the fulcrum of family activity. Bamboo has been planted along the flanks of the house to create a natural screen from the neighbouring property.

The 'journey' through the house employs cinematographic techniques to enhance the sense of discovery, exposing and then withholding immediate access to some spaces. The interior is revealed not as a linear progression but as a series of options to ascend and descend, with surprising turns, backtracking and cul-de-sacs.

Entered from an open-fronted carport that extends the full width of the house, the principal circulation route, a wide walkway, runs off to the left, bifurcating to form a gallery overlooking the courtyard and stairs and then descending, first to the level of the family room and further to the dining and living areas. The kitchen and service spaces are arranged parallel to the walkway. Beyond the dining space an open terrace overlooks a landscaped valley to the north of the house.

An external stair descends further to a library and home office and, at the lowest level of the house, the guest suite. Back at the entrance lobby a stair ascends to the master bedroom at the upper level. This is a quiet retreat with a series of balconies and terraces giving views over the roof to the east, west and north, and views down to the house entrance.

The use of full-height windows results in a house that is remarkably light and airy. This adds a further dimension, bringing in natural ventilation and daylight. Air conditioning is consequently minimized. The family room has a curious tilted window echoing the roof's slope.

The X1 House is not a small house, but its size is not immediately apparent because the house embraces the topography and works with the site rather than imposing itself

upon the land. It stands out for its distinctive modern form, but it is not pompous or pretentious. 'The entrance conceals the slope from the front so effectively that visitors are amazed to find the structure descending through several levels to the internal courtyard, the living and dining quarters, and then into the landscaped garden at the rear,' explains architect Lim Teng Ngiom.

Lim completed his architectural education at the University of North London, and after working in the UK and with Kumpulan Akitek in Malaysia, set up his practice in 1989. He identifies most easily with ideas about contemporary architectural aesthetics. 'We were all', he says, 'influenced by the works of the modernist masters. Most of all I admire the works of Le Corbusier.' The architectural critic Kenneth Frampton has described Ngiom's work as 'Latter day European Purism filtered through the works of OMA, that surfaces with refreshing energy and sculptural authority, within a Malaysian context.'[1]

[1] Kenneth Frampton, 'From Where I'm Standing: A Virtual View', in Tan Kok Meng (ed.), *Asian Architects*, Vol. 2, Singapore: Select Publishing, 2001, p. 17.

Left The principal axis of the house, with a long view from the entrance to the rear garden.

Below left An external stair gives access to the rear garden and the guest suite, bypassing the family accommodation.

Below The dining area is raised above the reception space.

Right Broad overhanging eaves ensure protection from sun and rainfall.

Left The dynamic form of interlocking cubes clusters around the open-to-sky courtyard.

Right The designer makes extensive use of steel and timber.

Far right The entrance lobby and the stair to the master bedroom suite.

Below The journey through the house reveals multiple levels and many surprising turns and niches.

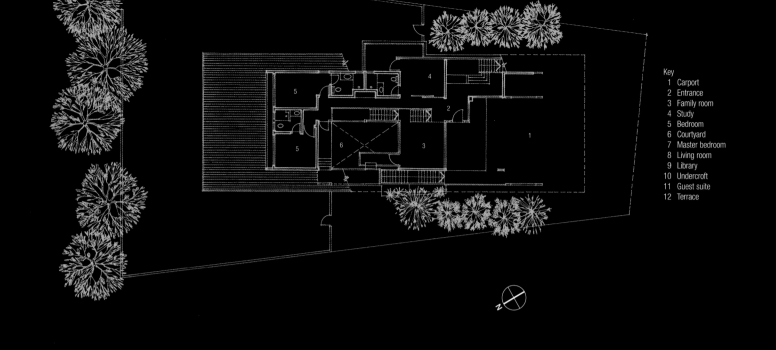

Key
1 Carport
2 Entrance
3 Family room
4 Study
5 Bedroom
6 Courtyard
7 Master bedroom
8 Living room
9 Library
10 Undercroft
11 Guest suite
12 Terrace

Above left Ground floor plan.

Left The X1 House has a distinctive modern form that sets it apart from its neighbours. The modest façade conceals a house that is large but does not dominate the site.

Above The rear balcony during a dramatic monsoon storm. Rainwater cascades into the valley below.

Below The section indicates the manner in which the house clings to the slope.

0   5   10 metres

X2 house

SIERRAMAS, SUNGAI BULOH, SELANGOR
ARCHITECT: LIM TENG NGIOM
NGIOM PARTNERSHIP

Lim Teng Ngiom, the designer of the X2 House, has tied his colours firmly to the mast of modernism. 'In today's global environment, I do not feel the need to consciously worry about working in an identifiable Asian context,' he has said. 'I believe in abstraction because it provides freedom…. I respond to climatic conditions because this provides reasons for the forms, and I believe in technology because that is the only way we can move forward.'

The X2 House is the second in a series of houses by Lim designed to explore the boundaries between interior and exterior, to produce 'pure white architecture' and to exploit light in its various manifestations.

The precedent for the innovative design is an earlier residence designed by Lim and completed in 1999. Known as Pat's House,[1] it was subsequently published widely and was much admired by Kuok Khoon Ping who commissioned the X2 House. The client subsequently proved to be a remarkable patron, passionate about architecture, open to new ideas and keenly interested in every aspect of the evolving design.

The X2 House sits upon a fan-shaped site, 45 metres deep, that falls 9 metres from west to east. Ten metres wide at the entrance, the plot expands to 35 metres at the lower boundary. The plan of the house responds directly to the site configuration and has developed as a series of triangulated shards or elongated rhomboids attached to a central rectangular spine.

Most of the accommodation is at ground floor level in a linear sequence, commencing with the wet kitchen and open-plan dry kitchen, leading to the dining area and the sitting area, thence to a library with the master bedroom and second bedroom-cum-study preceding two palatial bathrooms. The living room is a separate rhomboid-shaped pavilion 'bolted on' the north side of the house. The principal entrance to the house is on the north façade, with an entrance door that gives direct access to the sitting area.

The presence of water was an important requirement of the brief, and consequently water features flank the house. To the south of the dining room is a 10-metre-long triangular-shaped 'plunge' pool, and to the north of the dining area a linear *koi* pond. Yet another water feature appears below the terrace to the east of the living room.

A broad timber-floored terrace projects from the southern flank of the house and cantilevers out at the eastern extremity, over the sloping hillside. Like the earlier Pat's House, the external walls tilt outwards beneath the overhanging eaves, and the façade incorporates extensive glass louvres. The long narrow plan form assists in natural cooling,

Pages 136–7 The house exploits a steep slope with a composition of 'pure white architecture and light'.

Above Cantilevered monopitch roofs and tilting walls provide shaded interiors.

Right The house is a linear composition of open-plan spaces. View from the library to the dining area and kitchen, with the entrance from the carport beyond.

with the prevailing wind able to pass through the porous skin of the building.

The roof is in the form of a wide monopitch canting gently upwards at the eastern end with a separate monopitch above the carport at the western end. Horizontal metal eaves, steel balustrades, louvres and tiled boundary walls reinforce the linear emphasis in the design. A vertical water tower alongside the carport punctuates the sculptural composition and anchors the house to the land.

Tucked beneath the floor slab, at lower ground floor level, is a guest suite and a third bedroom. They share a broad shaded terrace looking east. As with the X1 House (page 126), the exploration of the house in cross section was vital in ensuring privacy, security and connectivity.

Innovative design has been central to Lim's evolving practice and he was instrumental in setting up the School of Architecture at Universiti Malaya (with Professor Ghauth Jasmon) in 1994–5. Lim reverses the notion that designing houses is a young architect's first step prior to designing larger corporate structures. His career began with large-scale projects such as factories and commercial buildings, and he has 'graduated' to smaller houses into which he invests intense energy and research.

1 Robert Powell, *The New Asian House*, Singapore: Select Books, 2001, pp. 64–9.

Above left The external walls of the house tilt outwards and incorporate glass louvres for natural ventilation.

Above The open-to-sky bathroom provides the sensuous experience of showering beneath the stars.

Key
1 Carport
2 Entrance
3 Living room
4 Dining room
5 Kitchen
6 Pavilion
7 Bedroom
8 Terrace
9 Plunge pool
10 Library
11 Guest suite
12 Terrace

0   5   10 metres

0   5   10 metres

Opposite above Plan at entrance level and section through the principal rooms.

Opposite below A separate monopitch roof covers the carport. The vertical water tower anchors the sculptural form.

Above and right The upper floor thrusts out beyond the lower terrace. At the lower level is a guest suite and maid's accommodation.

Left Detail of the boundary wall.

fathil house

MINES RESORT, KUALA LUMPUR
ARCHITECT: KEN YEANG
TR HAMZAH & YEANG

air mass and consequently provide thermal insulation, permeable façades addressing the prevailing northeast– southwest winds to give natural ventilation, openings on opposite sides of the central space capable of being adjusted to create a 'venturi' effect and water as a cooling device – but otherwise a well-mannered, somewhat restrained vocabulary with strong simple forms and clean lines that respond pragmatically to the context.

Like many recent large villas in Kuala Lumpur, the Fathil House is located in a gated development designed around a golf course. The house is entered from the southwest across a forecourt paved with Islamic-inspired patterns. On plan, two orthogonal forms slide against each other opening up a triangular void – a chasm linked by a slender bridge. A planar wall imposes a strong axis that is reinforced by the line of a gallery at first floor level and extends through the living space to emerge as a series of stepping stones across the 15-metre swimming pool. Alongside the entrance a narrow strip of water flows northeast and then returns through 180 degrees and terminates at a small *surau* (prayer room).

The two-storey living room is the focus of the house, a central space framed by two more solid elements that direct the eye northwards. The east wing of the house contains the master bedroom and a suite occupied by the owner's parents, interspersed with a home office, an audio-video room and a roof courtyard. The west wing contains the children's rooms above the kitchen, dining room and service areas. A second rooftop courtyard links the children's rooms. All relate to the central space and the dramatic bridge and staircase.

The house enjoys a panoramic view from the living room through tall sliding glass doors across the pool, to the golf course. The landscaped fairways and the forested hills on the horizon become 'borrowed space' and are a visual extension of the private living room.

Ken Yeang is the only Malaysian architect who has achieved an international profile comparable with the likes of Norman Foster, Kisho Kurokawa, Richard Meier and Zaha Hadid. Yeang's hard-won reputation was built upon a series of ground-breaking ecologically responsive buildings in the 1990s, namely Menara Mesiniaga in Subang Jaya (1992), Menara UMNO in Penang (1998) and the Guthrie Pavilion in Selangor (1998). This reputation was cemented with the acclaimed Singapore National Library (2003). Today, Yeang operates from two offices – his long-standing practice in Kuala Lumpur in partnership with Tengku Robert Hamzah and, since 2005, his London-based practice Llewelyn Davies Yeang.

The Fathil House was designed for a director of the company that commissioned the award-winning Menara Mesiniaga office building, but it does not display the same expressive façade details as the seminal high-rise tower, which was the recipient of an Aga Khan Award for Architecture in 1994. The ecological features are understated: correct orientation in relation to the sun path, a dynamic oversailing winged roof in the form of folded metal plates to provide shade, a tall central atrium to create thermal

Pages 144–5 The principal external feature of the house is the dynamic oversailing roof formed with metal folding plates.

Above A private roof garden with outdoor bathroom accessed from the master bedroom suite.

Right The house has a dignified architectural language with simple strong forms.

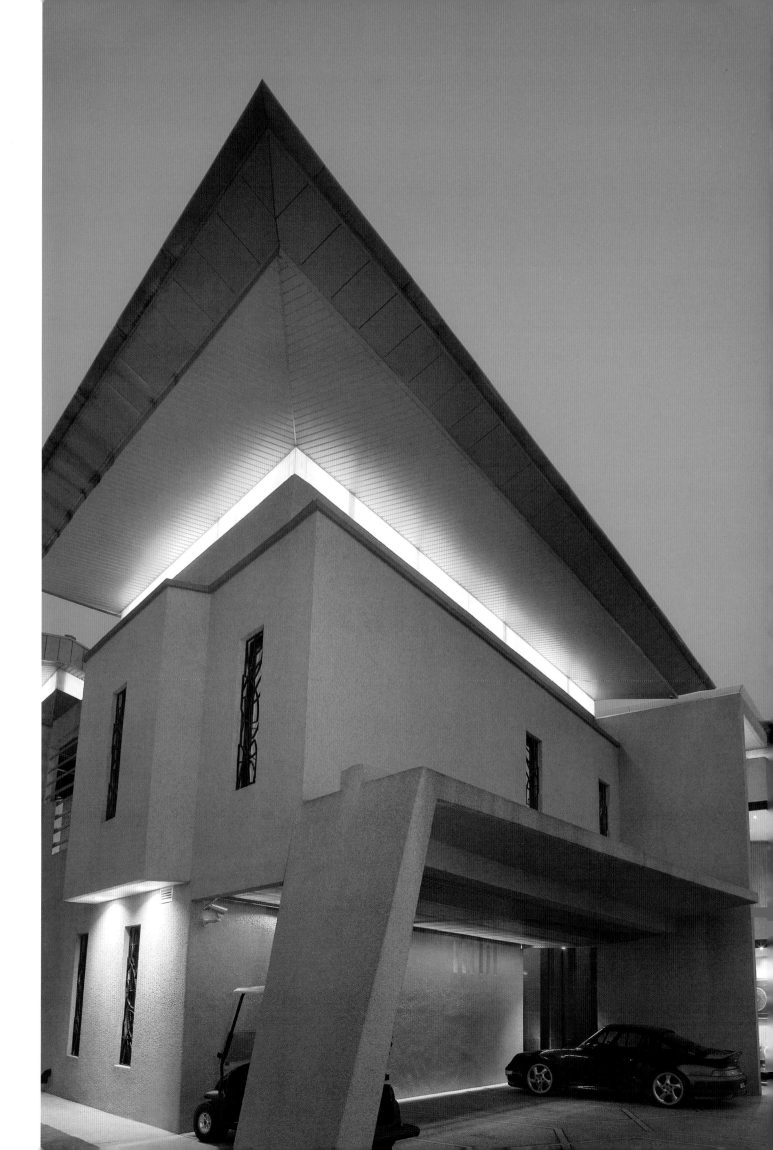

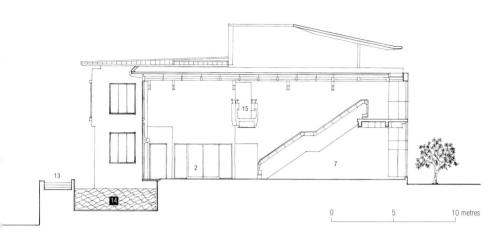

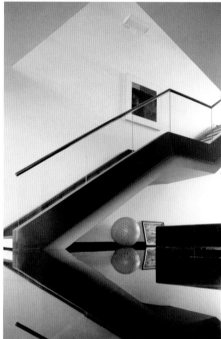

Pages 148–9 The dramatic two-storey living space is the focus of the house. A slender bridge links the two 'wings'.

Top left Section through the living room and pool.

Top Large openings at the rear face the prevailing winds.

Above The elegant staircase is a prominent element in the spatial composition.

Left The house is an impressive composition of light, space and structure.

Above The living room doors frame a vista over the swimming pool to the golf course and the forested hill beyond.

Right Ground floor plan.

Key
1 Entrance
2 Living room
3 Dining room
4 Office
5 Audio-video room
6 Parents' room
7 *Surau* (prayer room)
8 Kitchen
9 Carport
10 Maid's room
11 Laundry
12 Storeroom
13 Pool deck
14 Swimming pool
15 Bridge

wong soo house

SIERRAMAS, SUNGAI BULOH, SELANGOR
ARCHITECT: JIMMY CS LIM
CSL ASSOCIATES.

In the late 1980s Jimmy CS Lim designed a number of innovative dwellings in Kuala Lumpur that refocused the development of private residential architecture in Malaysia. The Eu House (1987) was closely followed by the Precima House (1988). Each detached residence was a radical reinterpretation of traditional vernacular dwellings. Lim holds firm convictions about what is appropriate architecture for the tropics and he is an outspoken opponent of what he terms 'the uncritical proliferation of Western temperate models of domestic architecture in the Southeast Asian context'.

Another house designed by Lim, the seminal Salinger House (1993), confirmed him as the leading proponent of contemporary vernacular approaches to the design of dwellings in the equatorial region. The significance of the Salinger House was recognized beyond Malaysia and in 1998 it received an Aga Khan Award for Architecture.

The Wong Soo House at Sierramas is similarly a transformation of a traditional vernacular model into a contemporary form. The unusual feature of the brief was that the owner of the house required a residence built around a fish pond. The fish – some 200 Japanese carp or *koi* species – were to be the focus of the house.

The exterior of the house gives little indication of its internal complexity. The main structure facing the estate road is a two-storey concrete frame with brickwork infill and with multiple clay-tiled roofs. The formal entrance is via a curved staircase not unlike that encountered in the *anjung* (entrance porch) of a Melakan courtyard house. Within the

house the materials, the scale and the mood change, with extensive use of timber for construction. Many of the details are developments of experimental timber construction in Lim's own home.

Lim has designed the house as a series of pavilions linked by timber bridges and shaded walkways, with vantage points to sit and observe the fish, places to handfeed them and other niches to sit in quiet contemplation. The pond at the heart of the dwelling is special; the dark waters will suddenly erupt as gold, bronze, orange, silver and red fish surge upwards to collect food thrown from the bridge. Their scales flash in the sunlight and a million tiny droplets of water catch the light. It is not difficult to understand the owner's fascination with the carp species *Cyprinus carpio* that is native to Japan and the temperate regions of Asia.

Each pavilion contains a specific function – living area, sitting area, library and formal dining room – and all overlook the water. The pavilions are of varying heights, each suited to their purpose, and with different floor levels so that the timber walkway that skirts the edge of the pond has slight

Pages 152–3 The house is a series of pavilions designed around a large *koi* pond. The traditional forms are evocative of a coastal Malay *kampung*.

Left There are numerous vantage points from which the owner can view his collection of over 200 Japanese carp.

Above Timber details developed by the architect in his own residence are applied extensively in the Wong Soo House.

Left The three-storey atrium at the heart of the dwelling enhances natural ventilation and filters sunlight.

Below The timber-clad pavilions are linked by a walkway, a reminder of Malaysian fishing villages such as Kukup.

variations in level. The walkways throughout evoke memories of fishing villages at Kukup on the west coast of Malaysia and of Kampung Ayer in Bandar Seri Begawan, Brunei Darussalam.

Embedded within the plan is a soaring atrium that assists in the natural ventilation and also filters light into the interior of the house. Each pavilion is separately roofed with half-round clay tiles so that the compound resembles a small *kampung*. Plants and shrubs are located between the pavilions and the car park is concealed in the basement.

Jimmy CS Lim was born in Penang and graduated from the School of Architecture at the University of New South Wales, Australia. He returned to Malaysia in 1978 to start his own practice. From 1991 to 1993 he was President of the Malaysian Institute of Architects (PAM) and he is an active conservationist and advocate of sustainable architecture. His practice in a shophouse in Jalan Scott, Kuala Lumpur, became something of a 'rite of passage' for young architects in the 1980s and 1990s and five of the designers featured in this book – Chris Lee, John Bulcock, David Chan Weng Cheong, Wooi Lok Kuang and Pilar Gonzalez-Herraiz – worked at some time for CSL Associates.

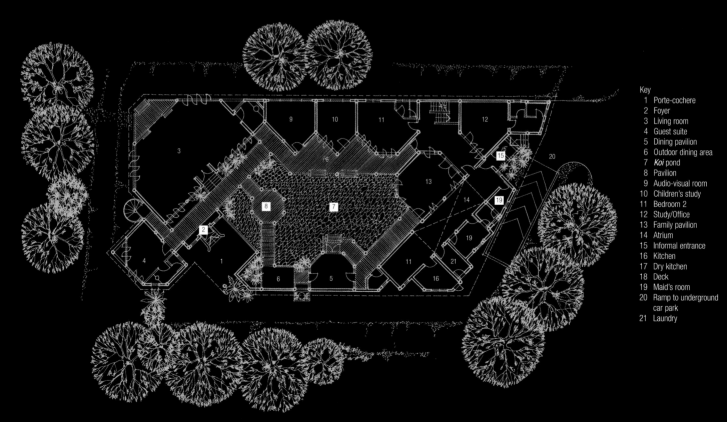

Key

1 Porte-cochere
2 Foyer
3 Living room
4 Guest suite
5 Dining pavilion
6 Outdoor dining area
7 *Koi* pond
8 Pavilion
9 Audio-visual room
10 Children's study
11 Bedroom 2
12 Study/Office
13 Family pavilion
14 Atrium
15 Informal entrance
16 Kitchen
17 Dry kitchen
18 Deck
19 Maid's room
20 Ramp to underground
   car park
21 Laundry

0   5   10 metres

Left The exterior of the house is 'closed' and secure, giving no hint of the 'openness' of the interior.

Below left Ground floor plan.

Right The formal entrance is via a curved staircase similar to that encountered in the *anjung* (entrance porch) of a Melakan courtyard house.

Below left Intricate timber joinery details are the hallmark of houses designed by Jimmy Lim.

Below right Multiple roofs are similarly a feature of the architect's oeuvre.

pixie house

LAKEVIEW BUNGALOWS, SAUJANA RESORT, SHAH ALAM
ARCHITECT: JOHN BULCOCK
DESIGN UNIT

Pages 160–1 The Pixie House is a stunning sculptural composition utilizing a language of horizontal and vertical planes juxtaposed against light-filled voids.

Below Views into the delightful central water court are tightly choreographed.

Opposite The living room projects into the water court and is visually connected to the dining room.

The essence of architecture is space – space that communicates to us at an individual level. Architecture must encourage contact with landscape, with nature and with place and, ultimately, contact with ourselves.' JOHN BULCOCK

John Bulcock has worked for more than a decade in Malaysia. A graduate of the Hull School of Architecture, UK, he acknowledges the influence on his early career of the landscape architect Per Gustavson and the former National University of Singapore lecturer Michael Woodcock who both taught at Hull. Bulcock arrived in Southeast Asia via India where he worked for two years with Balkrishna V. Doshi, who proved to be an important mentor. It provided a link with two of Bulcock's architectural heroes, Le Corbusier and Louis Kahn, for Doshi is one of the few architects to have worked for both of the modern masters.

Upon his arrival in Kuala Lumpur in 1994, Bulcock gained employment with Jimmy CS Lim, but his work first came to the attention of a wider audience with the publication in 2000 of a regional headquarters for the Danish firm Novo Nordisk.[1] The circular form designed by Bulcock and Hans Carl Jacobson is a sophisticated industrial building that combines the language of modern architecture with traditional responses to climate, and it marked the architect out as an emerging talent. He subsequently set up his own consultancy, Design Unit, in 2002.

The Pixie House is located at the intersection of two roads in Lakeview Bungalows, Saujana Resort, a gated residential development in Shah Alam. The trapezoid-shaped site enabled the architect to experiment with interlocking geometries, resulting in a north-facing E-shaped plan where the western leg has been rotated at 30 degrees to enclose a triangular courtyard and a water garden.

The house is entered directly from the street. An off-form concrete wall forms a visual barrier, and an abrupt turn brings the visitor into a reception area at the foot of the main staircase. The concrete wall is washed with light at night, directing the eye to the tall timber entrance door. The stair core is expressed externally on the southern façade with a cantilevered vertical slab of grey lava rock.

The principal circulation route within the dwelling is a broad central walkway running east to west, and perpendicular to this spine is the rectangular living room projecting north into the water garden. A dark reflective pool tumbles over a small waterfall into a lower pool. Contained by the living, dining and reception spaces, the higher-level water garden with a single tree is perceived as an outdoor room. The corner glass screens in the living and dining rooms slide away to create visual and spatial communication between the spaces across the water. Views into the central garden are tightly choreographed and the world beyond the boundary walls is consciously excluded. There is duality in the plan arrangement, with the external façades signalling enclosure

Right The glazed circulation spine on the upper floor connecting the master bedroom suite to the remainder of the family accommodation.

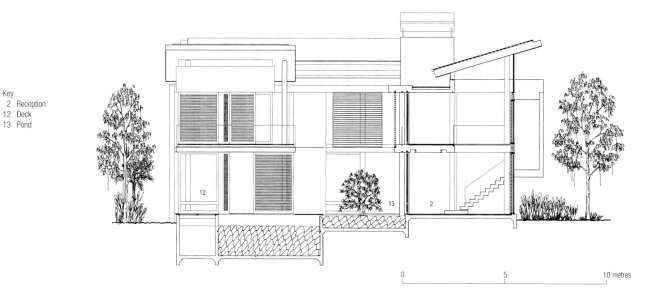

Key
2 Reception
12 Deck
13 Pond

0   5   10 metres

Top Section through the entrance lobby and the water court.

Above The elegant staircase with a glass balustrade springs from a black marble base.

Opposite The complex geometry of the plan is a direct response to the corner site at Suajana Resort. There is a masterly interplay of light and space.

and security and the interior façades conversely designed to be permeable and open.

To the west of the living room, the circulation route deflects at 20 degrees, leading past the guest suite to the side entrance. The principal family rooms are to the east of the living room – a formal dining room, a family dining space and an audio-visual room – together with wet and dry kitchens and ancillary service rooms.

On the upper floor of the Pixie House, the master bedroom suite, together with a studio and a roof garden, are accorded a degree of extra privacy. They are located at the western end of the house, separated by a glazed walkway from the family room and the children's bedrooms. The separation of function is emphasized by the geometry of the plan. At roof level these functions are expressed as six distinct roofs.

The Pixie House is essentially an inward-looking dwelling. Perimeter landscaping is intended to complement the rectilinear structure and to add another layer of security, while the palette of materials is restrained – off-form concrete, white painted render and natural anodized aluminium louvres. Titanium-zinc roof flashings conceal flat black concrete roof tiles. Cross-ventilation is an essential part of the design, and multiple louvred screens are designed to regulate the airflow, control solar radiation and exclude mosquitoes. Thrusting through the roofline is a glass and steel wind chimney that ventilates the house using a 'stack system'. The house is a stunning sculptural object utilizing a modern language, yet responsive to the climate and local culture.

[1] Robert Powell, 'Tropical Danish', *Steel Profile*, No. 80, 2002, pp. 14–17.

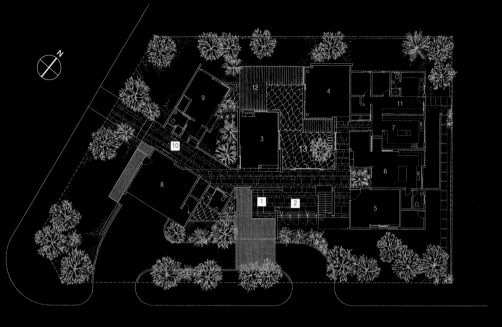

Key
1 Entrance   7   Wet kitchen
2 Reception   8   Garage
3 Living room   9   Guest suite
4 Dining room   10 Side entrance
5 Audio-visual   11 Laundry/Utility
   room   room
6 Family dining   12 Deck
   area/Kitchen   13 Pond

0   5   10 metres

Left Ground floor plan. The trapezoid-shaped plan relates to the site boundaries.

Below The house is inward looking, with all the principal rooms overlooking the water court.

Right above and below The restricted palette of materials includes off-form concrete, exposed steel and timber.

louvrebox
house

GITA BAYU, KUALA LUMPUR
ARCHITECT: KEVIN LOW
SMALLPROJECTS

The site for the Louvrebox House is a steeply sloping rectangular plot 15 metres wide and 36 metres long running north to south within a gated community at Gita Bayu. Kevin Low's response was to design a 'shoebox'-shaped house 5 metres wide, 25 metres long and 10.5 metres high. The challenging terrain played a fundamental role in the architectural solution but the starting point for the design was the traditional *kampung* house. The initial idea was to set the building on stilts, effectively freeing the area beneath the house for landscape. The undercroft has subsequently become living space but the strength of the initial *parti* is still apparent.

The orientation of the house is ideal because the long elevations face north and south and consequently the architect did not have to deal with direct sunlight in the morning and evening. Kuala Lumpur's location, just three degrees north of the equator, means that in the course of a year the house experiences sun from the south and from the north. The façades of the box are detailed according to their orientation. The east, south and west façades are protected by all-embracing screens of horizontal louvres made of powder-coated aluminium extrusions, while the north façade is essentially a solid masonry wall with recessed windows. Floating above the box is a monopitch 'ondoline' corrugated roof with substantial overhangs.

The duality in the plan is reflected in the arrangement of the interior. Service areas – bathrooms, dressing rooms, kitchen and service entry – are generally located on the north side of the box, while the living room, dining room, breakfast room and principal bedrooms face the south side overlooking a 2-metre-wide pool deck and a 17-metre-long trough-shaped lap pool that extend to the northern boundary. A 3-metre-wide landscaped strip runs parallel to the pool, providing shade at midday and privacy from the adjoining house.

The Louvrebox House was designed for a Swedish businessman and his Malaysian wife but in mid-2006 it was rented to an expatriate Australian family for whom the large 'outdoor room' in the form of the sun deck and lap pool was the focus of family activity.

The house is entered at the highest level of the site, directly from the street, thus permitting some interaction between private and public spaces. A setback of 6 metres provides space for two parking bays alongside the entrance, which is partially concealed behind a permeable vent-block wall. Brick walls screen stairs that descend on both sides of the house to the service yard and the pool deck.

Pages 170–1 Somewhat sombre by day, the Louvrebox House is transformed in the evening into a magic lantern.

Left The south, east and west façades of the house are protected from solar gain by horizontal sliding aluminium louvres.

Above The living room was originally conceived as an open space beneath the house. Subsequently enclosed, it enjoys an agreeable microclimate alongside the pool.

The entrance door gives access to a transparent glass tower embracing a staircase in the form of post-tensioned concrete wafers. The stair tower ascends through four storeys and fulfils a secondary function as a 'chimney', allowing air to rise, thus creating a 'stack' effect to dispel heat.

The narrowness of the one-room-wide plan also helps in this respect; by opening windows on the north and south elevations, through-draughts are encouraged. Adjusting the size of the window openings creates a 'venturi' effect where positive pressure builds up in the lee of the house and effectively promotes air movement. The lap pool also aids cooling and the creation of a satisfactory micro-climate alongside the principal living areas.

The appearance of the Louvrebox House changes dramatically as night falls. In daylight the louvred walls appear almost solid and relatively sombre, but as darkness descends and lights are switched on the house becomes a magical lantern and attains the transparency of a Miesien

box – an uncompromising modern dwelling. Low has produced what Anoma Pieris, his contemporary at MIT and now
a lecturer in architecture at the University of Melbourne,
has described as 'a gritty, yet sensitive vocabulary for a
modernist vernacular'.[1]

[1] Anoma Pieris, 'Kevin Low', in Philip Goad, Anoma Pieris and Patrick Bingham-Hall,
New Directions in Tropical Architecture, Singapore: Periplus Editions, 2005, p. 183.

Above A glass tower contains
the vertical circulation elements.

Below Section through the
garden court.

Right The 17-metre lap pool is in
the form of a concrete 'trough'.
Water spills over the end wall to
be recycled.

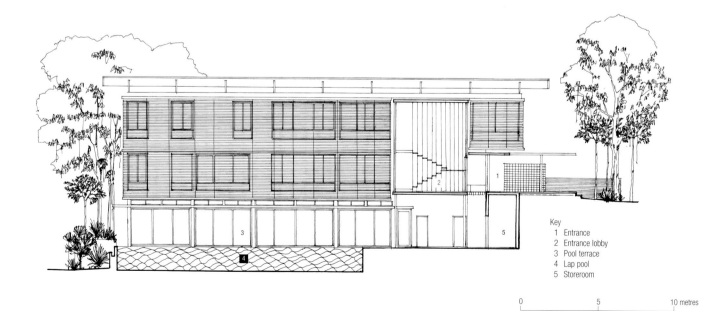

Key
1 Entrance
2 Entrance lobby
3 Pool terrace
4 Lap pool
5 Storeroom

0   5   10 metres

Above The glass staircase tower promotes natural ventilation.

Right The beautifully detailed open-riser staircase is suspended on steel rods.

Opposite top Plan at entrance level.

Opposite below left A bamboo grove along the southern boundary gives protection from overlooking by neighbouring houses.

Opposite below right Detail of aluminium louvres.

Key
1 Entrance
2 Entrance lobby
6 Carport
7 Master bedroom
8 Dressing room
9 Master bathroom
10 Audio-visual room

refurbished houses

bilis house

KUALA LUMPUR
ARCHITECTS: JOHN DING & KEN WONG
UNIT ONE DESIGN

John Ding and Ken Wong, the partners of Unit One Design, are graduates of the Welsh School of Architecture at Cardiff, UK. Their initial architectural education was influenced by Professor Patrick O'Sullivan, a renowned environmental scientist, who gave them an excellent technical background and, in Ding's words, taught them 'how to build'. Professor Ivor Richards mentored their final design thesis projects. After serving their apprenticeship in the office of ORMS Design and Architecture in London, Ding and Wong returned to Malaysia where they worked with TR Hamzah & Yeang and GDP Architects, respectively, before setting up Unit One Design in 1996.

One architect who has influenced their approach to design is Carlo Scarpa, and Ding and Wong seek to emulate Scarpa's mastery of tectonics, specifically the junction of materials.

The Bilis House is an example of that most ubiquitous form of Malaysian dwelling, the terrace house. Yet, it is a terrace house like no other for it has been so radically reconfigured and internally modified that in its reincarnation it bears little resemblance to its former self or to its neighbours.

Thin projecting canopies, horizontal black louvres, black painted rolled steel joists (RSJ's), circular hollow section (CHS) tubes and steel weldmesh screens clothe the original

Pages 178–9 The family room in the Lee House (page 188), as yet unfurnished, is a glass-sided pavilion adjacent to the pool.

Pages 180–1 In the refurbished Bilis House internal walls have been removed to create an uninterrupted flow of space.

Above The minimalist white interior of the dining area contrasts with the patio beyond.

Right Steel structure and white planes form a sculptural composition alongside the house entrance.

façade with a double-height 'second skin' – an exquisitely detailed black and white Mondrian-like mask. A smooth grey zinc titanium membrane has replaced the clay-tiled roof.

Jointly conceived by Ding and Wong, who work closely on all projects, the design of the Bilis House was driven by the desire for flexible living space. All the ground floor internal walls have been removed and replaced by judiciously located square hollow section (SHS) steel columns to create an uninterrupted spatial flow. This openness is accentuated by the fact that there are no doors, with the exception of the main entrance and the rear service entrance, both of which are made to look like simple pivoted planes. There are similarly few walls at first floor level and doors are concealed, with hidden hinges and handles.

The rear elevation has also been modified; the external wall has been removed and replaced by a tall, hinged, expanded metal screen that creates a direct link to a forestry reserve at the rear of the house. The reserve effectively becomes a visual extension of the living room – it is 'borrowed space'. The house colonizes the land at the rear and the steel grill simultaneously provides security and a controlled vista. When required, on social occasions, the steel mesh door can be thrown open and family and guests can spill out into the rear courtyard.

The architects' radical intervention in the Bilis House and the manipulation of space and light within the parallel party walls have the effect of making a modest dwelling appear considerably larger than it really is. It is also a highly personalized statement of the individual within a standard mass-housing typology.

Above left A tall, hinged, expanded metal screen provides security to the rear patio.

Above Horizontal black metal louvres ensure privacy for the otherwise transparent street façade.

Left The interior of the house has been transformed by the removal of internal partition walls.

Above and below Projecting canopies, exposed steel joists, horizontal aluminium louvres and expanded metal screens distinguish the house from its neighbours.

Opposite The modest terrace house has been radically reconfigured into an exquisite piece of modern architecture with an intriguing combination of transparency and concealment.

Far left The detailing of the junction of materials is exemplary.

Left The terrace house looks directly into the forest reserve at the rear. The forest effectively becomes 'borrowed space' and an extension of the living space.

Below The ground floor plan and section demonstrate the openness of the reconfigured plan and section.

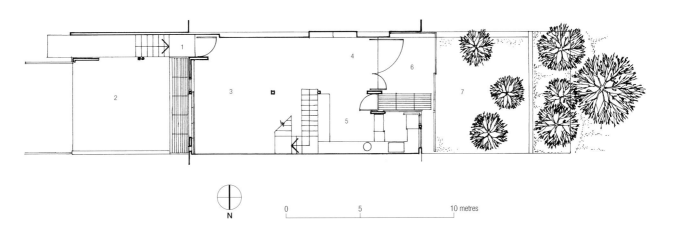

0   5   10 metres

Key
1 Entrance
2 Carport
3 Living room
4 Dining room
5 Kitchen
6 Patio
7 Courtyard
8 Bedroom

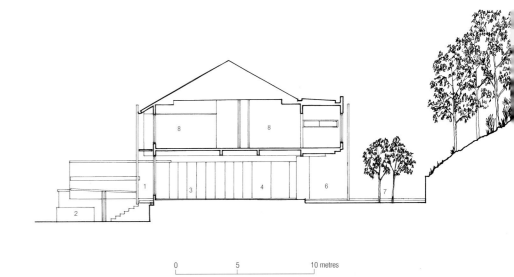

0   5   10 metres

lee house

DAMANSARA HEIGHTS, KUALA LUMPUR
ARCHITECT: CHRIS LEE
JELUTONG DESIGN

The Lee House is located on a steep hillside in Damansara Heights. The house modifies and extends an older family dwelling designed by Wells and Joyce (architects of the Kuala Lumpur General Hospital) in the 1960s. A high stone wall faces the road, giving the initial impression of a fortified entrance. An iron gate slides smoothly aside to provide access to an underground parking lot from which one ascends by a staircase that emerges at a roofed terrace, enclosed by an iron grille for security purposes. Less agile guests may choose to take an elevator to the ground floor reception space where chairs are formally arranged around a low table.

The darkness of the basement is in sharp contrast to the ground floor where sunlight glints on the surface of an open-to-sky water court flanked by the reception area. With the sliding doors open, the sound of a fountain pervades the house.

An underlying order becomes evident. The house is essentially a series of layers; five linear layers run along the hillside intersecting with four distinct horizontal levels that relate to the topography to form a matrix. At basement level the emphasis is on enclosure and high security; at the topmost level the emphasis is on openness, transparency and light. The layering orchestrates the transition from the public to the private areas of the house. The built form and section work with the topography and the climate to encourage cross-ventilation and passive cooling.

Slicing at right angles through this matrix is a central circulation axis, a 'processional route' ascending through the horizontal layers and connecting the various spaces. It appears as a bridge spanning the two-storey void above the dining area, linking the family room to the library and master bedroom and connecting the vertical circulation (staircases and elevator) at the front and rear of the dwelling.

Christopher Lee, who designed the house for his mother, trained at Cambridge University School of Architecture, UK, and worked with Llewelyn Davies (now Llewelyn Davies Yeang) and Eric Parry before returning to Southeast Asia in 1993. He set up C'Arch Architecture + Design with Chris Wong and practised in Kuala Lumpur before moving to Singapore to

work with Kerry Hill Architects. Kerry Hill was a huge formative influence on Lee, and the notion of a strong diagram underlying the design as well as the idea of the *promenade architecturale* are two aspects of Kerry Hill's work that have found their way into Lee's repertoire. 'Kerry composes tropical houses from one-room-wide rectangular blocks,' says Lee. 'I loved the simplicity of the blocks with depth and layered richness coming from the way the blocks related to each other through the semi and fully outdoor interstitial spaces. This way of composing houses is particularly suited to the tropics.'

Lee returned to Kuala Lumpur in 1999 and briefly worked with Jimmy CS Lim before setting up his own practice, Jelutong Design Inc., the same year. He now lives and practises in the US and has designed a number of residential projects in upstate New York.

The various 'events' in the Lee House are arranged perpendicular to the circulation axis. At ground floor level one progresses from the reception area to the formal dining room and thence to the sitting room and beyond to the visitors' suite. The interstitial spaces bring the different parts of the house into play with each so that one always has a sense of what is going on in other parts of the house.

Pages 188–9 The refurbished house shortly after completion. The family room is a glass-sided pavilion parallel to a 12-metre-long swimming pool.

Opposite The emphasis is on openness, transparency and light.

Above The house is capped with an inverted hemispherical roof above the artist's studio.

Ascending to the first floor, the family room is revealed as a glass-sided pavilion parallel to a 12-metre-long swimming pool and Jacuzzi that occupy a flat terrace carved from the hillside. This is truly the 'heart' of the house, an informal area with views over the terrace. The pool, which is fringed by banana palms and other trees, is a remnant of the former house on the site and holds many happy memories for the family.

At this point the circulation route doubles back to the master bedroom suite, the library and two smaller bedrooms. The bedrooms can be isolated at night by secure doors inspired by Peranakan screens. Paintings, ceramics and exquisite antique Chinese furniture punctuate the route through the house. A private staircase within the study leads to the rooftop and culminates in an artist's studio with stunning views across a turfed roof garden and raintree canopies to the Petronas Twin Towers – a view that visually connects the house to the ever-changing skyline of the city. It is a delightful retreat, a place to sit at sunrise or in the cool evening breeze.

Lee's architectural heroes include Le Corbusier, Marcel Breuer, Balkrishna Doshi and Graig Elwood, and the architectural language employed in the Lee House shows some evidence of their influence, with white planar surfaces and roofs expressed as horizontal lines floating above glass walls. The house is firmly planted on a stone podium and is capped by an inverted hemispherical roof above the studio.

Left The formal dining room and the reception area adjoin the water court.

Above At dusk there is an entrancing view from the roof garden of the changing skyline of Kuala Lumpur.

Right Section through the pool deck and principal rooms.

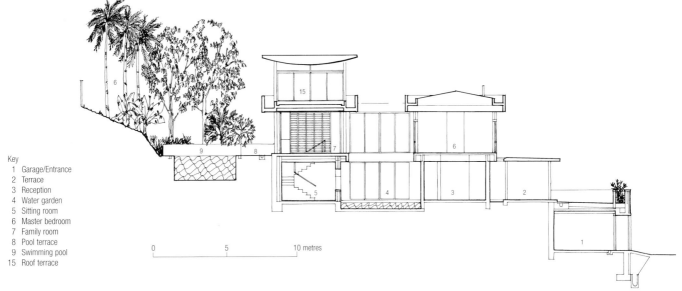

Key
1 Garage/Entrance
2 Terrace
3 Reception
4 Water garden
5 Sitting room
6 Master bedroom
7 Family room
8 Pool terrace
9 Swimming pool
15 Roof terrace

0   5   10 metres

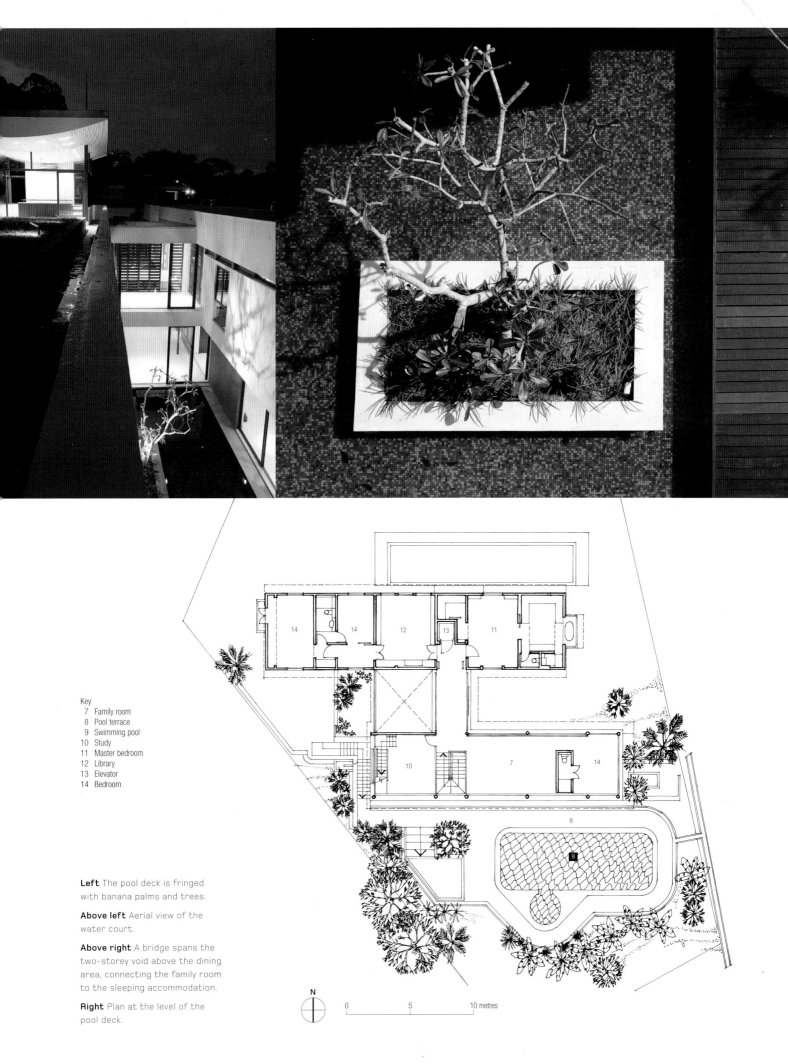

Key
7 Family room
8 Pool terrace
9 Swimming pool
10 Study
11 Master bedroom
12 Library
13 Elevator
14 Bedroom

Left The pool deck is fringed with banana palms and trees.

Above left Aerial view of the water court.

Above right A bridge spans the two-storey void above the dining area, connecting the family room to the sleeping accommodation.

Right Plan at the level of the pool deck.

N

0   5   10 metres

jalan tempinis satu house

BANGSAR, KUALA LUMPUR
DESIGNER AND LANDSCAPE ARCHITECT: NG SEKSAN
SEKSAN DESIGN

Ng Seksan, the principal of Seksan Design, gained a degree in civil engineering at the University of Canterbury in Christchurch, New Zealand, before changing tack and qualifying as a landscape architect at Lincoln University in Canterbury. His early designs were influenced by Martha Schwartz, particularly the American guru's use of unconventional landscape materials and her ability to work with topography, in the process blurring the lines between art and architecture. Later, Ng would be captivated by the work of Geoffrey Bawa, on one occasion taking his entire office staff to Sri Lanka to visit Lunuganga, the magical garden created by Bawa at Bentota.

The Jalan Tempinis Satu House was initially a bachelor residence and Ng's office when he set up his landscape practice in 1994. Now it is home to the designer, his wife and three small children, a live-in maid and two dogs (the office has meanwhile expanded and moved to larger premises). It is a house that has continuously evolved and grown by accretion over a period of some twelve years, and it has been the testing ground for many of Ng's ideas on space and materials. Today, it bears little resemblance to the original house built in the 1960s.

Ng Seksan professes only a passing acquaintance with Christopher Alexander's book *Pattern Language*, but the design of this house is a compendium of 'patterns' that would fit easily into Alexander's notion that there are timeless patterns embodied in the way mankind constructs its habitat. One such pattern is located immediately opposite the entrance to the house where a huge log lies parallel to the street. What at first seems to be the remains of a

Pages 196–7 The family home of Ng Seksan is constantly evolving. The house is a compendium of 'patterns' that would fit well into Christopher Alexander's notion of timeless spaces.

Left The robust construction of the original house has permitted constant remodelling of the internal space.

Above Art and architecture are closely related.

Right The house contains the works of several of Malaysia's most renowned artists.

Left Numerous reconfigurations of the original 1960s house have created a collage of spatial experiences.

Right Traditional glass louvres provide natural ventilation and daylight.

fallen tree awaiting removal is an astute response by Ng to a perceived need for a place for neighbourly interaction. Older folk use the log to sit and chat when taking their evening walk, parents bide their time there awaiting the school bus and drivers waiting for their employers rest here. In the process, the log has become an important piece of informal street furniture.

The house compound is entered through a narrow gate almost concealed by a tall *pulai* tree (*Alstonia angustiloba*) and other vegetation. Directly ahead and up a short flight of steps is a modest entrance door. Alongside the door a low timber deck projects into the forecourt – a second pattern – the equivalent of the shaded open-sided verandah (*serambi*) found in traditional Malay *kampung* houses. Its purpose is for greeting guests or for an informal conversation with a neighbour.

Once inside the house myriad patterns are encountered that are interwoven to create a rich tapestry of experiences: a fish pond with water spilling over the lip of a huge clay pot, a walled garden with tall slender Assai (*Euterpe oleraccea*) and Macarthur (*Ptychosperma macarthurii*) palms and a richly tactile floor of bricks and pebbles, an elevated children's play pool, a shaded timber verandah, a wall of books, a sunroom, a hammock, a conservatory, a traditional Malay baby sling suspended from a beam by a rubber cable, and a family sleeping deck with two large mattresses beneath a slowly revolving fan. The spaces give the impression of gradual evolution, of response to change and to the growth of the family. The boundary between interior and exterior is, as in the best houses in the tropics, ambiguous – an in-between space. The boundary between functions is similarly ambiguous, a step in the floor level or a lowered ceiling sending a subtle signal.

Works of art play an important role in the interior design of the house and are visible everywhere. The collection contains the work of some of Malaysia's most renowned artists. Some of Ng's work takes inspiration from experi-mental art works which are translated into landscaped parks and gardens.

The house is located on a sloping site and the entrance is at ground floor level. A flight of stairs descends to a sub-basement floor. There is thus a distinct horizontal separation between the private family spaces on the ground floor and the more public spaces at the lower level where guests are entertained.

Geoffrey Bawa's influence is evident in the framing of views into courtyards, the placing of objects as the focus of internalized vistas, and most memorably, the climb to the roof of the house to encounter a small garden and a 'love seat' to enjoy quiet contemplation surrounded by purple bougainvillea (*Elizabeth Angus*), white 'cat's whiskers' (*Orthosiphon aristatus*), purple 'amazon blue' (*Octacanthus caeruleus*), red *Kalanchoe blossfeldiana* and yellow blooms of the *Coreopsis* tickseed species beneath the evening sky – a reminder of the rooftop of Bawa's town house in Bagatelle Road in Colombo.

But the dwelling is more than physical space. It is also about the manipulation of light and materials: sunlight angling through the trees onto the brick-paved courtyard or shimmering on the surface of the pool, of ficus climbing fair-faced concrete. The house is challenging for the designer's children who learn to live with nature, to negotiate ladders, to have no fear of water; in the process, it becomes a repository of their memories.

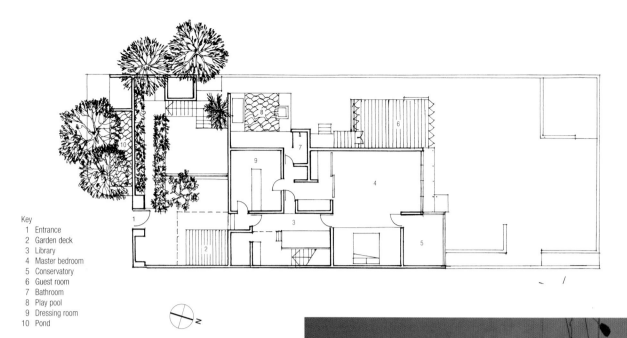

Key
1 Entrance
2 Garden deck
3 Library
4 Master bedroom
5 Conservatory
6 Guest room
7 Bathroom
8 Play pool
9 Dressing room
10 Pond

0   5   10 metres

Above Plan at the entrance level.

Below Detail in the bathroom.

Right The narrow entrance gate beneath a *pulai* tree brings visitors to a low timber deck not unlike the traditional Malay *serambi* where guests are greeted.

Left The top-lit dining area overlooks the landscaped courtyard.

Above There are artworks in every nook and cranny.

Below The children's playroom opens out to the sunken courtyard at the rear of the house.

second homes
and retreats

serendah
house

SERENDAH, RAWANG
ARCHITECT: ABDUL HARIS BIN OTHMAN
RDA-HARRIS ARCHITECTS

The small township of Serendah lies north of Kuala Lumpur on the road to Ipoh. Here, the house of architect Abdul Haris Bin Othman and his wife Liza Abu Bakar clings to the summit of a hill overlooking the fairways of the Serendah Golf Resort.[1]

When Haris commenced the design of the house, almost everyone he knew was into Balinese or Thai 'style'. He reasoned this was merely a passing fad inspired by a plethora of style books, and he wanted to design a house that would have a modern form while employing traditional materials and details. He did not want the house to be explicitly 'Malay' or 'Malaysian' but he did want it to overtly convey its origins.

The design takes an unusual form. At the highest point on the site is a square tower. This forms an anchor for the plan that radiates out from one corner of the tower with a structural frame cantilevering out over the precipitous slope. Haris explains the house as 'an exercise in horizontal and vertical planes to define space. The heavy mass of the tower contrasts with the light and airy ambience of the living spaces and the open decks.' The design is site-specific and is intended to capitalize on the special qualities of the location – the surrounding trees and views of the golf course and the distant hills. The existing trees provide shade and are utilized as windbreakers, for as Haris remarks succinctly, 'It can get quite windy up here.'

The house is not for those who suffer from vertigo since the forested topography plunges almost vertically below the living room. The upside is that the house enjoys spectacular views and is continuously cooled by the prevailing breeze.

The living area is at ground floor level and is contiguous with a TV area on a raised timber platform. Another room, in the ground floor of the tower, is designated as a library but its excellent acoustics have made it the preferred venue for the owner to play his saxophone. It is where Haris, a former Colombo Plan scholar and graduate of the University of South Australia School of Architecture at Adelaide, jams with invited guests at the weekend. In the first floor of the tower is a guest bedroom.

Adjoining the living area is an open-plan kitchen and breakfast bar. The emphasis is on informality, with activities shifting in the course of the day much as they do in a traditional Malay *kampung* house where the different areas are defined by slight changes in floor level. A wide external verandah skirts the house at the level of the surrounding treetops. There is an outdoor terrace where the owner likes to relax before dinner.

One level below is the master bedroom, the study, a second bedroom, bathrooms and walk-in dressing rooms with an external deck that gives access to the swimming pool. This too is poised on the sloping hillside. One further level down is the pool filtration equipment and other service spaces.

The roof of the house expresses the central stabilizing purpose of the corner tower. The principal roof members radiate out from this point and the roof slopes outwards

Pages 204–5 The three-storey Enderong House (page 216) sits on soaring stone-clad columns on the side of a steep hill.

Pages 206–7 At the highest point of the site is a square tower with an inverted hemispherical roof.

Above The roof structure radiates from the corner tower.
The entertainment area is on
a platform slightly raised above
the fan-shaped living room.

Above A secluded corner of the house conducive to contemplation and reflection.

Opposite The heavy mass of the tower, which anchors the dwelling to the site, contrasts with the light and airy ambience of the living spaces and cantilevered decks.

and down to the perimeter, with wide overhanging eaves that shed rainwater without the use of gutters into the surrounding forest. The sloping roof is an exposed timber structure covered with hardwood shingles. The main staircase that rises through four floors is constructed of steel and timber and is similarly tied firmly to the central structure.

Large open *pelantar* (decks) with simple seating platforms or *pangkin* are provided. A variety of openings – windows, timber grilles, roof gaps and louvres – provide maximum cross-ventilation and hot air is drawn upwards, to be dispelled through the tower.

The precedence for the form of the house and the external language is beguiling. Haris explains that it is simply a romantic house that emanates in part from his appreciation of modern architecture in the West, but there are also memories evoked of a childhood spent in Sarawak and the vernacular dwellings of the Bidayuh people. The indigenous Bidayuh occupied timber houses raised on wooden piles that made extensive use of *resak* timber, which has many of the qualities of *chengal*. They also used *belian* timber shingles. Both timbers are used extensively in the Serandah House. Haris sees the special allure of his residence arising from the intimate relationship it enjoys with nature. All the senses are gratified, distant hills and greenery provide visual pleasure and the cool breezes give relief from the energy-sapping humidity of the city. The silence in the forest is a great aid to relaxation.

Haris set up RDA-Harris Architects in 1995. Prior to that he was principal architect of Kuala Lumpur City Centre (KLCC) and architect-of-record for the Petronas Twin Towers, at that time (1992) the world's tallest building. His work now includes master planning and urban design, often employing Islamic planning and design principles, such as the *chahrbagh* at Cyberjaya. His practice has garnered a host of awards, but the house at Serendah is perhaps the most enduring personal statement of his architectural philosophy.

[1] Robert Powell, 'A Romantic House', *d+a*, Issue 7, Singapore: SNP Media Asia, 2002, pp. 42–6.

Above A broad external verandah skirts the house at treetop
level. For the owner, the house
evokes memories of the vernacular dwellings of the Bidayuh
people of Sarawak.

Right The master bedroom and
associated terrace enjoy magnificent views of the golf course
and forested hills beyond.

Right An infinity pool with stunning views of the tree canopy.

Above The house is located on the crest of a hill overlooking the Serendah Golf Resort.

Left Plan at the entrance level.

Opposite above left An open-riser staircase leads to the summit of the tower.

Opposite above right The mass of the tower contrasts with the permeable open decks.

Right Section through the tower and principal rooms.

0   5   10 metres

Key
1 Carport
2 Guardhouse
3 Studio roof garden
4 Library
5 Entrance
6 Kitchen
7 Utility room
8 Breakfast deck
9 Verandah
10 Living room
11 *Pangkin* (raised platform)
12 Pool
13 Deck
14 Study
15 Maid's room

0   5   10 metres

enderong house

TANARIMBA, JANDA BAIK, PAHANG
ARCHITECT: NGAN CHING WOO
CWN ARCHITECTS

Pages 216–17 The Enderong House rises on stone-clad columns from the deeply incised valley of the Sungai Enderong at Janda Baik, 35 kilometres north of Kuala Lumpur.

Left The house is embraced by the forest and has a low carbon footprint.

Right Locally sourced materials are used in furthering the designer's sustainable construction agenda.

The moving spirit behind the master plan is architect Patrick Ngan Ching Woo of CWN Architects. Ngan is fulfilling a lifelong dream at Janda Baik. In 1964, after graduating in architecture from University College Dublin, he undertook graduate studies in landscape architecture at the University of Pennsylvania under Professor Ian McHarg, the renowned Scottish-born author of *Design with Nature*. The ecologically sound principles imparted by McHarg have remained with Ngan throughout a career that has taken him from a lectureship at the National University of Singapore School of Architecture (1969–72) at a time when there were many politically active students on campus, to a directorship with Akitek Antara Sdn Bhd, and finally to CWN Architects, a practice he set up with Choo Gim Wah in 2001. Ngan is also Managing Director of the development company Sitrac Corporation Sdn Bhd, which is spearheading the Tanarimba project at Janda Baik.

The Enderong House was one of the first houses to be completed on one of the designated 0.405-hectare lots, with a utopian vision rivalling Frank Lloyd Wright's decentralized Broadacre City for single detached dwellings. The three-storey house, with its extensive undercroft, reaffirms the ecologically sensitive principles underlying the whole development. It sits on soaring stone-clad columns, clinging to a 1 in 2.5 slope above the Sungai Enderong, with minimal use of retaining walls.

The house is built with predominantly locally sourced materials. All of the stone and 70 per cent of the timber used in the construction were recycled from on-site excavation and felling of trees required for the access road, while trunks of *chengal, merbau and meranti bukit* felled many years ago by illegal cultivators and left on the forest floor were used for rafters, flooring, window frames and doors. All combine to produce a contemporary vernacular language. Kitchen cupboards, bed frames, tables, stools and lamp bases were built from recycled pine logs.

Janda Baik lies 35 kilometres northeast of Kuala Lumpur on the Karak Highway to Kuantan and close to the hill resort of Genting Highlands, both in the state of Pahang. Tanarimba at Janda Baik is a far-sighted plan that encompasses 2913 hectares of hilly terrain rising from 450 metres to 1350 metres above sea level, with deep valleys, fast-flowing mountain streams and several 12 to 18-metre-high waterfalls. The plan identifies approximately 20 per cent of the land for development, with 80 per cent earmarked for retention as primary forest reserve to be managed and maintained for education, research and eco-tourism. Three peaks, Bukit Repin (1340 metres), Gunung Sempah (1205 metres) and Bukit Bankong (1041 metres), fall within the plan as does Genting Bedai, otherwise known as 'The Gap', part of an historic trail linking Kuala Lumpur to the east coast of Malaysia.

In a major departure from the prevailing construction practice in Malaysia, the roads and services within the development have been carefully designed to follow the contours in order to minimize earthworks and conserve as much as possible of the existing vegetation. Some 120 hectares of pine forest, planted in the 1970s by the Forestry Department, skirt the main highway. This area, known as 'The Pines', has the atmosphere of a temperate pine forest with 20-metre-tall pine trees thrusting skywards and little undergrowth.

Above High ceilings, wide over-hangs and shaded verandahs ensure the interior remains cool without the use of air conditioning.

Skilled local workers from the nearby town of Bentong carried out the robust details. Roof tiles, rafters, floor-boards and joists are exposed in their natural state. High ceilings, wide overhangs and shaded verandahs ensure that air circulates freely and the interior remains cool without the use of air conditioning. The temperature at 580 metres above sea level is a cool 20–27 degrees, whereas in Kuala Lumpur on the same day it is 32 degrees.

This is a dwelling in harmony with its natural surroundings. From the open terraces there are panoramic views of the forest. In the valley below, the river has been diverted to create a fish pond and bathing pool. Wildlife sighted in the forest reserve includes gibbons, honey bears, wild boar, hornbills, rare white-crested eagles, owls and a host of smaller birds.

Tanarimba at Janda Baik offers an alternative lifestyle in a development driven by Ngan's desire to build a sustainable community that has minimal impact on the environment.

Right The privacy of the site location permits an outdoor bathroom with extraordinary views over the surrounding hills.

Above The breakfast area and kitchen open out to a timber-floored verandah.

Below Light fittings are custom-made utilizing locally sourced timber.

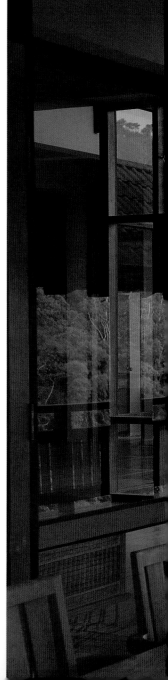

Right The house at night with the family in residence.

Below The external dining area with a timber deck extending out into the forest.

0   5   10 metres

Left Plan at living room level indicating the broad timber deck.

Below The house is located in relatively undisturbed primary forest.

Right Section through the Enderong House.

sum sum valley house

TANARIMBA, JANDA BAIK, PAHANG
ARCHITECT: CHOO GIM WAH
CWN ARCHITECTS

The Sum Sum Valley House is the second home of business-woman Ungku Dolly binti Ungku Abdul Raman and her husband Neil Duckett, a graduate of the AA School of Architecture who is a photographer, film maker and media consultant. Duckett admires the work of the Bauhaus, Gerrit Rietveld and Marcel Breuer, and he and his wife gave very clear direction as to their preferred architectural idiom. They wanted an uncomplicated modern concrete and glass structure (seemingly transparent) in the midst of the forest, a dwelling that would open up to breathtaking views of the valley.

Duckett provided the initial sketch plan and thereafter had a close working relationship with Choo Gim Wah of CWN Architects. Numerous design discussions were held and the house is the result of their close collaboration. Choo has an unusual background, first majoring as an economist and studio artist at the College of Wooster, Ohio, before switching to architecture and qualifying with a Masters of Architecture from Miami University of Ohio where he studied under Professor Jose Garcia and Professor Sergio Sanabria. He went on to work with Akitek Antara Sdn Bhd before setting up CWN Architects with Ngan Ching Woo in 2001.

While his partner is deeply wedded to timber as a material, Choo shares Neil Duckett's passion for concrete and glass. Choo's own architectural 'heroes' are Carlo Scarpa and Mies van der Rohe.

Located on a precipitous hillside above the Sum Sum River, the 0.644-hectare site is on the boundary of the forest reserve and tall trees climb the slopes behind the house. Designed as an uncompromising 27-metre-long, 7-metre-wide linear box in reinforced concrete and glass, the house straddles the 650-metre contour line on reinforced concrete piloti and micro piles. There is minimum interference to the topography and the vegetation as the house clings

tenaciously to the steep southeast-facing slope 25 metres above the fast-flowing river below.

The house dramatically terminates the winding road from the lower reaches of the valley. Cars are parked on a plateau four metres below the entrance and the final approach is via a broad flight of steps to arrive somewhat breathless at an airy glazed foyer at the lower ground floor level.

The house has an open-plan design with free-flowing space vertically and horizontally. A two-storey void links the living room on the ground floor to the family room on the first floor. Extensive full-height glazing maximizes the connection to the surrounding forest and also captures the natural light. Interior finishes include reflective 'honey-beige' marble and polished birch and *merbau* timber flooring.

Decks cantilever out 3.5 metres from the living room and dining room on the southeast façade, and the family room opens to a roof deck where the owners enjoy the cool outdoor climate and captivating forest views. Sliding doors on both sides of the one-room-wide plan permit cross-ventilation. The house is comfortable without air conditioning; indeed, it can be cold in the evening and a fireplace with an external steel chimney is incorporated in the living area.

There are no restrictions on the type of material that can be used in Tanarimba at Janda Baik but the design and

construction of the house are required to preserve the natural features. Fair-faced concrete is employed for the building exterior with natural anodized aluminium windows and mild steel railings. From the opposite side of the valley, the house is read as a series of horizontal planes, with an extraordinary transparency between the planes.

The orientation of the site nullifies potential problems of insolation, and thus the design of the Sum Sum House is essentially driven by the views and the topography. The house is at once utterly alien yet totally embraced by the verdant landscape.

Above Wide external terraces project in front of the living room and guest suite.

Above right The minimalist kitchen and dining area.

Right Extensive full-height glazing creates an immediate link between the house interior and the surrounding forest.

Key
1 Foyer
2 *Lanai*
3 Study
4 Entrance hall
5 Living room
6 Dining room
7 Kitchen
8 Guest suite
9 Terrace

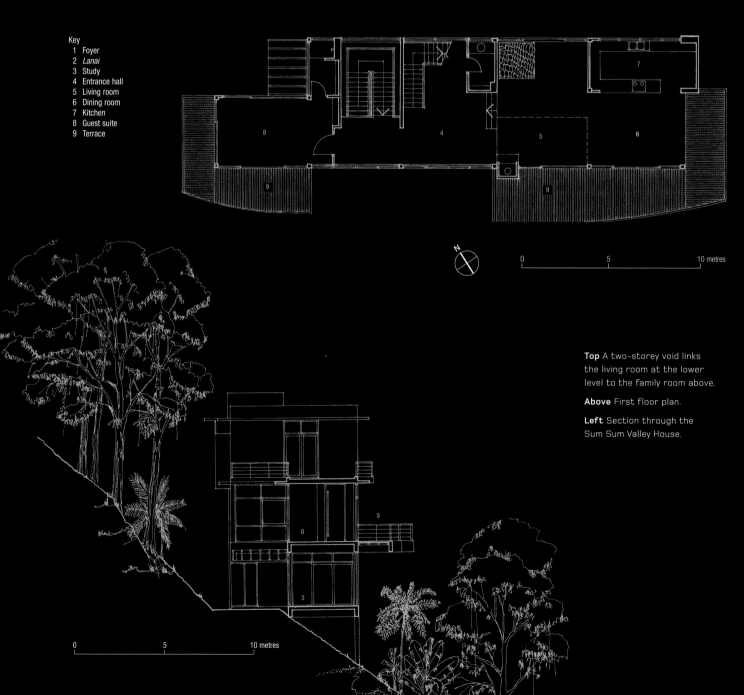

0   5   10 metres

0   5   10 metres

Top A two-storey void links the living room at the lower level to the family room above.

Above First floor plan.

Left Section through the Sum Sum Valley House.

Right Plan at entrance level.

Below From afar the house reads as a series of horizontal planes and has a distinctive transparency.

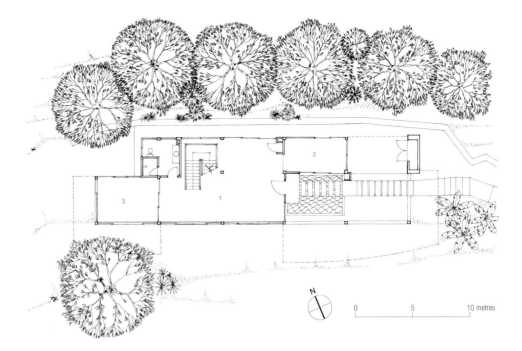

sekeping
serendah

SERENDAH, RAWANG
DESIGNER AND LANDSCAPE ARCHITECT: NG SEKSAN
SEKSAN DESIGN
WITH LAU JIAN PYNG, TAM MEI SIM, CAROLYN LAU & CHEW POH FOOK

'Sekeping Serendah is a personal experiment and demonstration of building on a steep vegetated site without destroying the land. It is a response to the slash-and-burn, cut-and-fill way of building in Malaysia. It also attempts to use the minimum member sizes for a simple dwelling. This involves a paradigm shift to a traditional view that a house is only a temporary shelter or tent ... and not a mini palace/monument.' NG SEKSAN

Sekeping Serendah is located some 40 kilometres north of Kuala Lumpur.[1] A minor road off the Kuala Lumpur–Ipoh highway skirts a lake and an abandoned quarry before becoming an unmade track hemmed in on either side by jungle. The track gently ascends, passing through an Orang Asli (Aboriginal) village where a dozen thatch-roofed timber dwellings are strung along the path.

The first indication of the house is the appearance of a visibly alien structure in the jungle – an iron gate set in a gabion wall. The gate slides smoothly aside to allow access to a clearing in the forest. A short journey on foot is then necessary, across an iron footbridge spanning a swift-flowing stream, and then on to the opposite side of the valley through dense vegetation. Suddenly, there it is, one moment imperceptible, the next an angular dark alien presence in grey steel and glass. Its substance is obvious, yet uncannily it is dematerialized – the glass skin reflects the forest and the building is a mirror of its surroundings. It is visible but at the same time invisible.

The house, one of two almost identical dwellings, is the creation of Ng Seksan who trained as a civil engineer in New Zealand before qualifying as a landscape architect. It is a weekend retreat from the metropolis for his family.

Basically, the house is a 5.5 square metre cube constructed from 100 mm x 100 mm 'I' beams and 100 mm x 100 mm square hollow section steel posts with 20 mm steel cables providing cross bracing. The cube is carried upon five steel pilotis that raise it above the steeply sloping valley floor, and it has a monopitch roof. The cube is divided laterally into a raised ground floor with a ceiling height of 3.5 metres and a first floor with a soffit that follows the slope of the roof and rises from 2 metres to approximately 3.5 metres. The steeply sloping roof has wide projecting eaves in order to shed the monsoon rain, and both the roof and side walls are clad in Zincalume custom orb profile.

The austere nature of the primary structure is continued in the secondary elements. The ground floor is composed of 3 mm mild steel sheets painted with epoxy paint while the first floor is covered with 250 mm-wide *resak* timber planks from the local hardware store. (Ng describes *resak* as the poor man's *chengal*).

Pages 234–5 Sekeping Serendah is located in primary forest 40 kilometres north of Kuala Lumpur.

Opposite Sited in an isolated valley, the steel and glass pavilion has a close relationship with nature.

Above Detail of the galvanized industrial metal deck and the perimeter timber bench.

Above The dwelling exhibits an ambiguous edge between interior and exterior, a hallmark of the best houses in the tropics.

Left The galvanized metal deck is accessed from below by a ladder. The opening is sealed at night.

Below Elevation.

Right Tall windows in the living area and kitchenette open directly to the surrounding jungle.

Key
9 Swimming pool

9

0   5   10 metres

The ground floor is a single-volume living space with a small kitchenette in one corner. The first floor is similarly a single-volume space for sleeping. Projecting from the ground floor and overlooking the valley is an outdoor living space constructed from galvanized industrial metal grating, surrounded by a timber bench and flanked by a timber day bed. This structure, which resembles in scale and function the traditional *serambi* (verandah), is carried on additional pilotis. The house is entered via a steep steel staircase through a void in the floor, which gives access to the outdoor living space. At the rear of the cube is an open-to-sky bathroom with an outdoor shower. Constructed of locally manufactured clay bricks, the bathroom sits on a concrete slab that is partly suspended and partly on excavated ground. Fresh water is obtained from a stream on higher ground and gravity-fed, electricity is supplied from the national grid with overhead cables from a substation a kilometre away, while sewage goes into an underground septic tank. The space beneath the house is used for storage.

Sekeping Serendah is a modern take on a jungle hut in a thickly forested valley. Life is reduced to the essentials, and notwithstanding the use of modern technology it is very much in the spirit of a traditional dwelling. The house has a special relationship with nature. Totally isolated in a cleft in the terrain, a deep silence reigns, broken only by the sound of water tumbling over rocks and tree roots. At night the forest retreat is magical. In the deep blackness, one sleeps surrounded by the sound of insects. At dawn sunlight slants through the forest canopy and dances on the surface of the pool in the forest clearing.

Raising a house above the forest floor is a traditional response to give protection from intruders, both human and animal. It ensures that the house is dry during flash floods following the monsoons and that breezes flow beneath and through the dwelling. The Orang Asli employ minimal timber posts and woven *attap* thatch to create porous structures, while the contemporary dwelling uses louvred Naco windows to achieve porosity – but the intention is the same. The house also shows the influence of contemporary houses in New Zealand and Australia, such as the Israel House at Paradise Beach in New South Wales by Peter Stutchbury. The juxtaposition of the old and the new is startling, as is the use of thousands of years of accumulated wisdom. The technology is minimal, based on instinct and experience rather than mathematical formulae.

Trees cut back during construction have grown aggressively to almost engulf the house and render it invisible. Urbanized man is never far from his primitive origins. And that is the beauty of Sekeping Serendah; it is at one with and coexists with nature. Perhaps, eventually, the forest will reclaim the site or, alternatively, it may be engulfed by the inexorable expansion of the city.

[1] Robert Powell, 'Dwelling in the Forest', *d+a*, Issue 18, Singapore: SNP Media, 2004, pp. 28–31.

Far left An underview of the steel deck projecting from the ground floor.

Left The outdoor bathroom. Showering outdoors is a sensuous experience.

Below The external deck, a modern version of the *serambi*, is the focus of social life when the owner is in residence.

Right The simple glass cube is surrounded by the forest.

Below right Plans of the two floors of the weekend house.

Key
1 Living area
2 Kitchenette
3 Bathroom
4 Day bed
5 Bench
6 Balcony
7 Bedroom
8 Deck
9 Outdoor living area

0   5

0   5   10 metres

mud
houses

SERENDAH, RAWANG
ARCHITECT: KEVIN LOW
SMALLPROJECTS
IN COLLABORATION WITH LAU JIAN PYNG
& NG SEKSAN

'Modern architecture should always be unfinished, allowing time to complete it.' KEVIN LOW

Two mud houses at Serendah designed by architect Kevin Low are particularly relevant to the exploration of the new Malaysian house. They are the most experimental of all the houses in this book in that they pioneer the use of adobe in the context of contemporary houses in Malaysia. Yet, they are the smallest and least 'complete' of the dwellings.

The two guesthouses are located on a northwest-facing slope deep in the forest 40 kilometres north of Kuala Lumpur, close to two steel-frame houses constructed two years earlier (see page 234). The owners, their families and guests spend weekends at the retreat and often, at dusk, around the barbecue, the discourse turns to ethical questions sometimes, but not always, about ecology and sustainability. In this context, was it a good thing to bring so many 'foreign' materials into the forest to build the steel houses? The haulage vehicles damaged the narrow roads leading past an Orang Asli village and the materials were expensive. Couldn't the forest supply the bulk of the materials? Mud is available in great quantities but is not used widely in Malaysia. Could the material be viable for low-cost housing?

And so began an experiment with laterite mud scoured from the hillside behind and tamped in timber formwork to form the main walls of the two houses. Adobe is widely used in other parts of the world, including Australia, Mexico and Africa, and Low was able to draw upon many examples.

Pages 242–3 The Mud Houses seek to achieve a zero carbon footprint using locally sourced materials.

Opposite In the valley below the houses, a swimming pool has been constructed, fed by a small stream.

Above The two dwellings are an experiment in the use of adobe in the Malaysian context. The 'living room' is an outdoor brick-paved terrace with a wide over-hanging monopitch roof.

Left A collage of elements: the sheltered outdoor terrace, the open-to-sky bathroom and, in front, the access road.

When pursuing his graduate studies at the Massachusetts Institute of Technology, Low's thesis mentor was Professor Ronald Lewcock who headed the Aga Khan Program dealing with the understanding of non-Western architecture. Low spent some two months with Lewcock in the ancient city of Sana'a in the Yemen. There he became familiar with the technology of building with timber and the use of stone, rubble and brick in house construction. The experience gave him an appreciation of clarity in structural expression and honesty in the use of materials. His experience of rammed earth was amplified by a workshop he carried out with Jody Gibbs, an architect from Arizona.

The work of Andy Goldsworthy, a British artist and sculptor, has also inspired Low. Most of Goldsworthy's work has been made in the open air, in places as diverse as the Yorkshire Dales in the UK, the Northern Territories of Canada, the North Pole and the Australian outback. Goldsworthy's goal is to understand nature by participating in it as intimately as he can. He generally works with whatever comes to hand: twigs, leaves, stones, snow and ice, reeds and thorns. Most works are ephemeral but demonstrate an extraordinary sense of place. Low finds these qualities fascinating and directly relevant to the production of architecture.

The two guesthouses at Serendah are perched on rising ground in the forest above a fast-flowing stream. Just two trees were sacrificed to create a level base. The simple rectangular plan includes sleeping quarters, bathrooms and an outdoor brick-paved terrace with a wide overhanging monopitch roof. The forest canopy provides shade. Materials used are locally sourced timber, laterite mud and corrugated cement sheeting for the roof. The mud walls are 400 mm thick and were compacted in four or five 'lifts' using timber formwork. A small amount of cement was added for longevity and better bonding. The upper part of each dwelling is a lightweight insect screen to permit cross-ventilation while excluding mosquitoes and geckoes. Parts of the external walls are sliding screens. Between the two houses is a space that will eventually become a secure play area for children. In the valley below, a stream has been diverted for use as a natural swimming pool. Cooking takes place outdoors on an iron griddle. The openness of the two houses is a reminder of the austere beauty of the Cinnamon Hill House at Lunuganga by Geoffrey Bawa.[1]

Also evident at Serendah is the influence of the work of the American landscape architect Martha Schwartz. Ng Seksan's earliest landscape works were inspired by the combination of fine art and landscape in Schwartz's designs, particularly her use of site-specific landforms as works of 'art'. These influences find expression here, notably in the pool projecting into the forest, a solitary steel mesh chair placed on a grassy knoll and an isolated Philippe Starck-style stool in a forest clearing. The unfinished houses are already acquiring a patina of age as the jungle seeks to reclaim territory.

[1] Robert Powell, 'The Cinnamon Hill House', in Robert Powell, *The Tropical Asian House*, Singapore: Select Books, 1996, pp. 30–7.

Far left and left Time measured by the shifting shadows cast on mud walls and brick paving.

Right Section through one of the Mud Houses.

Below The silence of the forest is disturbed only by the splash of water from a stream that has been diverted around the Mud Houses.

Below right A single modern steel chair encounter in a forest clearing gives pause for reflection on contemporary life and nature.

Key
2 Bedroom
3 Outdoor living area
5 Bathroom

Left A nearby Orang Asli dwelling. Much can be learned from 'architecture-without-architects' and the vernacular response to climate.

Below and right An open-to-sky bathroom in the Mud Houses.

Bottom The adobe walls merge with the jungle.

Above Only two trees were sacrificed to create a flat surface for the terrace – an exercise in sustainable construction.

Right The simple rectangular plan includes sleeping quarters and open-to-sky bathrooms.

Key
1 Entrance
2 Bedroom
3 Outdoor living area
4 Cloakroom
5 Bathroom
6 Children's play area

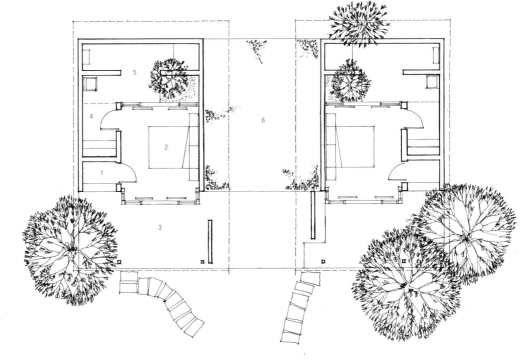

Select Bibliography

Abel, Chris, *Architecture and Identity*, Oxford: Architectural Press, 1997.

Baker, Philippa (ed.), *Architecture and Polyphony: Building in the Islamic World Today*, London: Thames & Hudson, 2004.

Chen Voon Fee (ed.), *The Encyclopedia of Malaysia: Architecture, Vol. 5*, Singapore: Archipelago Press, 1998.

Frampton, Kenneth, 'From Where I'm Standing: A Virtual View', in Tan Kok Meng (ed.), *Asian Architects*, Vol. 2, Singapore: Select Publishing, 2001, pp. 16–17.

Khan, Hasan-Uddin, 'The Architecture of the Individual House', in Robert Powell (ed.), *The Architecture of Housing: Exploring Architecture in Islamic Cultures*, Geneva: The Aga Khan Trust for Culture, 1990, pp. 165–83.

Knapp, Ronald G. (ed.), *Asia's Old Dwellings: Tradition, Resilience, and Change*, Hong Kong: Oxford University Press, 2003.

Lim Siew Wai, William and Tan Hock Beng, *Contemporary Vernacular*, Singapore: Select Books, 1998.

Lim, Vincent, 'Nothing But More', *d+a*, Issue 14, Singapore: SNP Media Asia, 2003, pp. 16–22.

London, Geoffrey, 'Earthly Paradise', *Monument*, No. 41, NSW, Australia, April/May 2001, pp. 76–81.

McGillick, Paul, *25 Tropical Houses in Singapore and Malaysia*, Singapore: Periplus Editions, 2006.

Norberg-Shultz, Christian, *Roots of Modern Architecture*, Tokyo: ADA Edita, 1998.

Pieris, Anoma, 'Kevin Low', in Philip Goad, Anoma Pieris and Patrick Bingham-Hall, *New Directions in Tropical Architecture*, Singapore: Periplus Editions, 2005, p. 183.

Powell, Robert, 'Architecture as a Palimpsest', *d+a*, Issue 10, Singapore: SNP Media Asia, 2002, pp. 40–3.

_____, *The Asian House: Contemporary Houses of Southeast Asia*, Singapore: Select Books, 1993.

_____, 'The Cinnamon Hill House', in Robert Powell, *The Tropical Asian House*, Singapore: Select Books, 1996, pp. 30–7.

_____, 'Dwelling in the Forest', *d+a*, Issue 18, Singapore: SNP Media Asia, 2004, pp. 28–31.

_____, 'A Fortified Haven', *SPACE*, February/March 2002, pp. 62–7.

_____, 'Introduction: Houses are Frequently the Most Powerful Indicators of Cultural Change', *IDEAS*, Vol. 2, Kuala Lumpur: Asia Design Forum Publications, 2006, pp. 8–12.

_____, *Ken Yeang: Rethinking the Environmental Filter*, Singapore: Landmark Books, 1989.

_____, *The New Asian House*, Singapore: Select Publishing, 2001.

_____, *The New Singapore House*, Singapore: Select Publishing, 2001.

_____, *The New Thai House*, Singapore: Select Publishing, 2003.

_____, 'Nuanced Materiality', *The Architectural Review*, No. 1265, UK, July 2002, pp. 82–5.

_____, *Rethinking the Skyscraper: The Complete Works of Ken Yeang*, London: Thames & Hudson, 1999.

_____, 'A Romantic House', *d+a*, Issue 7, Singapore: SNP Media Asia, 2002, pp. 42–6.

_____, *SCDA Architects: Selected and Current Works*, The Master Architect Series VI, Mulgrave, Victoria, Australia: Images Publishing, 2004.

_____, *The Tropical Asian House*, Singapore: Select Books, 1996.

_____, 'Tropical Danish', *Steel Profile*, NSW, Australia, No. 80, 2002, pp. 14–17.

_____, *The Urban Asian House: Contemporary Houses of Southeast Asia*, Singapore: Select Books, Singapore, 1998.

Powell, Robert (ed.), *Architecture and Identity: Exploring Architecture in Islamic Cultures*, Vol. 1, The Aga Khan Award for Architecture and Universiti Teknologi Malaysia, Singapore: Concept Media, 1983.

_____, *The Architecture of Housing: Exploring Architecture in Islamic Cultures*, Geneva: The Aga Khan Trust for Culture, 1990.

_____, *Modern Tropical Architecture: Line, Edge and Shade*, Singapore: Page One, 1997.

_____, *Regionalism in Architecture: Exploring Architecture in Islamic Cultures*, Vol. 2, The Aga Khan Award for Architecture and Bangladesh University of Engineering and Technology, Dhaka, Singapore: Concept Media, 1985.

Riley, Terence, *The Un-Private House*, New York: Museum of Modern Art, 1999.

Schaik, Leon van, 'SCDA Architects: A Review', *SIA-GETZ Architecture Prize for Emerging Architecture*, exhibition catalogue, Singapore, 2006.

Serageldin, Ismail, 'The Architecture of the Individual House: Understanding the Models', in Robert Powell (ed.), *The Architecture of Housing: Exploring Architecture in Islamic Cultures*, Geneva: The Aga Khan Trust for Culture, 1990, pp. 205–6.

Tan Hock Beng, 'Appropriating Modernity', *a+u*, Vol. 97:02, No. 317, Tokyo, February 1997, pp. 116–17.

Tay Kheng Soon, 'The Architectural Aesthetics of Tropicality', in Robert Powell (ed.), *Modern Tropical Architecture: Line, Edge and Shade*, Singapore: Page One, 1997, pp. 40–5.

Tur, Elias Torres, 'Thoughts about Architecture', in Phillipa Baker (ed.), *Architecture and Polyphony: Building in the Islamic World Today*, London: Thames & Hudson, 2004, pp. 146–7.

Yeang, Ken, *The Architecture of Malaysia*, Amsterdam: The Pepin Press, 1992.

Directory of Architects

Lurah Tunku House *(page 20)*
Bukit Tunku, Kuala Lumpur
and
Sadeesh House *(page 58)*
Subang Jaya, Kuala Lumpur

Architect: Ernesto Bedmar
B. Arch. (Cordoba), IAAA, ASIA
Bedmar and Shi Pte Ltd
12a Keong Saik Road
Singapore 089119
Tel: +65 6227 7117
Fax: +65 6227 7695
Email: bedmar.shi@pacific.net.sg
Web: www.bedmar-and-shi.com

Setiamurni House *(page 30)*
Bangsar, Kuala Lumpur

Architect: Chan Soo Khian
B. Arch., M. Arch. (Yale), AIA, MSIA, RIBA
SCDA Architects
10 Teck Lim Road
Singapore 088386
Tel: +65 6324 5458
Fax: +65 6324 5450
Email: scda@starhub.net.sg
Web: www.scdaarchitects.com

Bukit Ledang House *(page 40)*
Federal Hill, Kuala Lumpur

Architect: Kerry Hill
Kerry Hill Architects
29 Cantonment Road
Singapore 089746
Tel: +65 6323 5400
Fax: +65 6323 5411
and
30 Mouat Street
Freemantle
WA 6060
Australia
Tel: +61 9336 4545
Fax: +61 9336 4546
Email: kerry@kerryhillarchitects.com

Wooi House *(page 48)*
Shah Alam, Selangor

Architect: Wooi Lok Kuang
P. Arch., APAM, AIPDM, M. Arch. (NSW)
Wooi Architect
45-3A, Level 3, OG Business Park
58200 Kuala Lumpur
Malaysia

Tel: +603 7782 5518
Fax: +603 5192 9082
Email: wooiarch@tm.net.my

Safari Roof House *(page 66)*
Damansara Indah, Kuala Lumpur,
Louvrebox House *(page 170)*
Gita Bayu, Kuala Lumpur
and
Mud Houses *(page 242)*
Serendah, Rawang

Architect: Kevin Low
smallprojects
No. 1 Jalan Tenggiri
59100 Kuala Lumpur
Malaysia
Tel: +601 2200 1800
Fax: +603 2282 2861
Email: lsd@pd.jaring.my
Web: www.small-projects.com

Caracol House *(page 74)*
Kuala Lumpur
and
Tierra House *(page 100)*
Lakeview Bungalows, Saujana Resort,
Shah Alam

Architects: Frank Ling
AA Dip., M. Arch. (RMIT), RIBA, ARB
& Pilar Gonzalez-Herraiz
AA Dip., RIBA, ARB
**Architron Design Consultants
Sdn Bhd**
C-8 Taman Tunku
Bukit Tunku
50480 Kuala Lumpur
Malaysia
Tel: + 603 6204 2999
Fax +603 6204 4999
Mobile: 012 233 5687
Email: info@architrondesign.com.my
Web: www.architrondesign.com
and
6-C Paseo de la Habana 50
28036 Madrid
Spain
Tel: +34 630020243
Tel/Fax: +34 915641533
Email: pilar@architrondesign.com.my;
pilar-architron@telefonica.net

Lydia's House *(page 82)*
Kota Damansara, Kuala Lumpur

and
Ambi House *(page 92)*
Nilai, Seremban

Architects: Ar. David Chan Weng Cheong
B. Arch. (Curtin, WA), APAM, AIDPM
& Chan Mun Inn
B. App. Sci. (Arch.), B. Arch. Hons. (Curtin,
WA)
**DCA (Design Collective Architecture
Network)**
17A+B+C Jalan SS22/19
Damansara Jaya
47400 Petaling Jaya
Selangor
Malaysia
Tel: +603 7727 0199; +603 7727 2199
Fax: +603 7722 3199
Mobile: +601 2215 0311; +601 7333 3614
Email: muninn@dca.com.; mydavid@dca.com.my;
Web: www.dca.com.my

Johor House *(page 112)*
Leisure Farm Resort, Johor
and
Bilis House *(page 180)*
Kuala Lumpur

Architects: John Ding
BSc. Arch. (Hons.), B. Arch. (Hons.), RIBA
& Ken Wong
BSc. Arch. (Hons.), B. Arch. (Hons.), APAM,
RIBA
Unit One Design Sdn Bhd
18-3 Jalan 27/70A
Desa Sri Hartamas
50480 Kuala Lumpur
Malaysia
Tel: +603 2300 8200
Fax: +603 2300 8300
Email: john@unitone.com.my; ken@unitone.com.my
Web: www.unitone.com.my

X1 House *(page 126)*
Sierramas, Sungai Buloh, Selangor
and
X2 House *(page 136)*
Sierramas, Sungai Buloh, Selangor

Architect: Lim Teng Ngiom
BSc. (Hons.), Dip. Arch. Hons. (London),
MSc. (UM), APAM, IPDM
Ngiom Partnership
Suite D30, 3rd Floor, Block D, Plaza
Pekeliling

Jalan Tun Razak
50400 Kuala Lumpur
Malaysia
and
128 Jalan Cempaka Hutan
Sierramas
47000 Sungai Buloh
Selangor
Malaysia
Tel: +603 4043 4833
Fax: +603 4413 3833
Mobile: 012 288 5175
Email: ngiom@ngiom.com

Fathil House *(page 144)*
Mines Resort, Kuala Lumpur

Architect: Ken Yeang
AA Dip., PhD. (Cantab.), APAM, FSIA, RIBA,
FAIA (Hons.), FRIAS, FRS
Plym Professor (University of Illinois)
Adjunct Professor (Universiti Malaya)
TR Hamzah & Yeang Sdn Bhd
8 Jalan 1, Taman Sri Ukay
Jalan Ulu Kelang
68000 Selangor
Malaysia
Tel: +603 4257 1966
Email: kynnet@pc.jaring.my
and
Llewelyn Davies Yeang
Brook House, Torrington Place
London WC1E 7HN
UK
Tel: +44 (0)20 7637 0181
Fax: +44 (0)20 7637 8740
Email: l.chew@ldavies.com
Web: www.ldavies.com

Wong Soo House *(page 152)*
Sierramas, Sungai Buloh, Selangor

Architect: Jimmy CS Lim
B. Arch. (NSW), APAM, FRAIA, RIBA
CSL Associates
8 Jalan Scott
50470 Kuala Lumpur
Malaysia
Tel: +603 2274 2207/2274 2368/2274 2369
Fax: +603 2274 3519
Email: cslcyy9@tm.net.my
Web: www.jimmylimdesign.com

Pixie House *(page 160)*
Lakeview Bungalows, Saujana Resort,
Shah Alam

Architect: John Bulcock
Dip. Arch. (Hull), RIBA
Design Unit Sdn Bhd
Suite 829, 8th Floor, Sun Complex
Jalan Bukit Bintang
55100 Kuala Lumpur
Malaysia
Tel: +603 2141 5744
Fax: +603 2144 4659
Email: john@designunit.com.my

Lee House *(page 188)*
Damansara Heights, Kuala Lumpur

Architect: Chris Lee
MA, Dip. Arch. (Cantab.), ARB, APAM
Jelutong Design Inc.
2 Horatio Street #17A
New York, NY 10014
USA
Tel: +917 699 8639
Email: CFHLee@gmail.com
Web: www.jelutongdesign.com

Jalan Tempinis Satu House *(page 196)*
Bangsar, Kuala Lumpur
and
Sekeping Serendah *(page 234)*
Serendah, Rawang

Designer and Landscape Architect:
Ng Seksan
BE (Civil), Dip. LA, ANZILA, AILA (Malaysia)
Seksan Design
67 Jalan Tempinis Satu
Lucky Gardens
Bangsar
59100 Kuala Lumpur
Tel: +603 2282 4611; 2282 0366
Email: mail@seksan.com
Web: www.seksan.com

Serendah House *(page 206)*
Serendah, Rawang

Architect: Abdul Haris bin Othman
APAM, ARIA
RDA–Harris Architects Sdn Bhd
259 Jalan Ampang
50450 Kualu Lumpur
Malaysia
Tel: +603 4256 9906

Fax: +603 4253 2705
Email: rdaharis@streamyx.com;
harrisdoha@gmail.com

Enderong House *(page 216)*
Tanarimba, Janda Baik, Pahang

Architect: Ngan Ching Woo
B. Arch. (Dublin), MLA (Penn.), APAM, MSIA,
RIBA
CWN Architects
Lot 6.12, 6th Floor, Wisma Cosway
Jalan Raja Chulan
50200 Kuala Lumpur
Malaysia
Tel: + 603 2148 0611
Fax: +603 2148 3591
Email: cwnarch@streamyx.com

Sum Sum Valley House *(page 226)*
Tanarimba, Janda Baik, Pahang

Architect: Choo Gim Wah
BA (S. Arts and Econs. Hons.), M. Arch.
(Miami), APAM
CWN Architects
Lot 6.12, 6th Floor, Wisma Cosway
Jalan Raja Chulan
50200 Kuala Lumpur
Malaysia
Tel: + 603 2148 0611
Fax: +603 2148 3591
Email: cwnarch@streamyx.com

AUTHOR
Robert Powell
BA, Dip. Arch., M. Arch., RIBA, MRTPI, MSIP
Architect/Planner/Writer
R5 Marine Gate
Brighton BN2 5TN
UK
Tel: +44 (0)1273 624 855
Email: robertpowell42@yahoo.co.uk

PHOTOGRAPHER
Albert Lim KS
12 Koon Seng Road
Singapore 426962
Tel: +63 453 218
Email: albertlim55@yahoo.com.sg

Acknowledgements

In 1984 I was asked to edit the proceedings of a conference in Kuala Lumpur. I had recently taken up an appointment at the National University of Singapore and the invitation launched me on a new trajectory. The subject was 'Architecture and Identity', and it was the first in a series of seminars organized by the Aga Khan Trust for Culture on the challenges facing architects in the Islamic world. For the opportunities that the conference in Malaysia subsequently offered, I have to thank Suha Özkan, then Deputy Director of the AKAA, and Dato' Ken Yeang, at that time President of the Malaysian Institute of Architects (PAM).

A book has a life of its own. The seed of an idea may lie dormant for months, even years, then it germinates and takes off in directions that are not entirely predictable. And so it was with *The New Malaysian House*; the research and writing process became an exciting journey with unexpected encounters along the way. I have to thank several people who have assisted me. These include Abdul Haris bin Othman and Liza Abu Bakar, Ernesto Bedmar, John Bulcock, Chan Mun Inn, Chan Soo Khian, David Chan Weng Cheong, Cheah Kok Ming, Chew Poh Fook, Choo Gim Wah, Stefano Delisi, John Ding, Neil Duckett and Ungku Dolly binti Ungku Abdul Raman, Fathil Sulaiman bin Ismail, Foo Hwa Hin, Kerry Hill, John Hung, Joseph Khoo, C. H. Khor, Kuok Khoon Ping, Carolyn Lau, Lau Jian Pyng, Anderson Lee, Chris Lee, Puan Sri Irene Lee, John Lee, Lim Cho Wei, Jimmy CS Lim, Linda Lim, Lynda Lim Kwee Geok, Richard Lim, Lim Teng Ngiom and Melissa Lim, Frank Ling and Pilar Gonzalez-Herraiz, Ruby Loo, Low Chee Kiang, Kevin Low, David Mah, Mirzan Mahathir, Mohamed Shah, Mok Chee Paan, Ng Seksan, Patrick Ngan Ching Woo, Nor Azua Ruslan, Sadeesh and Smita Raghavan, Professor David Robson, Tan Mei Sim, Tang Hsiao Seak, Tengku Robert Hamzah, Wooi Lok Kuang, Eric Wong Weng Hoe and Ken Wong.

Kuala Lumpur is the birthplace of my wife Shantheni Chornalingam. I have to thank our extended family for their support while I was carrying out research in Malaysia in 2006 and our daughter Zara Shakira Powell for initial copyediting and for taking my photograph which appears on the back flap of the jacket.

I am indebted to Eric Oey, CEO and Publisher of Periplus Editions for undertaking the publication of this book and to Noor Azlina Yunus for her meticulous editing of the text.

Finally, I wish to acknowledge the contribution of my collaborator, the vastly experienced Singapore-based photographer Albert Lim Koon Seng. Albert has a keen eye, a steady hand, a wonderful unflappable temperament and total honesty, qualities I have come to value highly over the years.

Pages 254–5 Janda Baik offers the opportunity to escape the stress of city life, to relax, to enjoy the natural environment, to revitalize the body and to restore the soul.